# Catholic
# ANSWERS
## *for*
# Catholic
# PARENTS

St. Andrew's Productions

*McKees Rocks, PA*

# DEDICATION & CONSECRATION

To my beloved Spiritual father, Pope John Paul II. Truly he is Pope John Paul, the Great. To my mom, Trudy, for giving me the most precious gift of all: my Catholic Faith, and to Our Lady of Perpetual Help, the Mother of God who helped bring me home to the Faith!

ISBN: 1-891903-14-4

Distributed by:
St. Andrew's Productions
6091 Steubenville Pike, Bldg. 1, Unit #7
McKees Rocks, PA 15136

Tel:    412-787-9735
Fax:    412-787-5024
Web:   www.SaintAndrew.com

PRINTED IN THE UNITED STATES OF AMERICA

# Acknowledgments

To my dear husband, Michael, and my children, Corbin, Emilee, Shelbee, Mary, Catherine, Grace and Clare for putting up with me with patience and love as I had my nose glued to the computer screen for hours on end while producing this work; to Shelly Lembke, for going way above and beyond the call of duty and friendship in the initial editing process and to all my special friends who are moms and share my world of being a Catholic mom in the twenty-first century.

# Publisher's note

Special thanks to those who also assisted in the preparation of this book - Fr. Robert Hilz, Deacon Ray Helguson, Clyde Gualandri, and Michael Fontecchio.

# About the Author

A popular speaker and lecturer to Catholic Mothers, Maria Compton-Hernendez, M.Ed., is the author of three books, including the Catholic Bestseller, *The Catholic Mothers Resource Guide*, (Riehle Foundation). Her other recent release is, *Catholic Parents Internet Guide* (St. Andrew's Productions).

Maria is the web author of *The Catholic Mother's Internet Connection* website, which has won the Catholic Family Site Excellence Award. Maria is also the owner of J.M.J. Products, a successful internet-based business specializing in Catholic products.

Maria, along with her husband Michael, have six children, Corbin, Emilee, Shelbee, Mary-Therese, Catherine, and Grace. They reside in Kansas.

You may visit the J.M.J. website directly at:

www.totallycatholic.com

Visit the Catholic Mother's Internet Connection at:

www.catholicmothers.com

Send e-mail directly to Maria at:

Sales@totallycatholic.com

# FOREWORD

I am happy to recommend this easy-to-use reference book by Maria Compton-Hernandez on some sixteen topics that many Catholic parents can find helpful in understanding and explaining to their children and others about the Catholic Faith.

These sixteen topics range from the Holy Eucharist to the Dogmas about the Blessed Virgin Mary, Papal Infallibility, and the importance of chastity. It concludes with an explanation of relics, sacramentals and saints. These topics confuse many of people. However, these topics need to be seen in light of the whole revelation of God to His Holy People, called and redeemed by the Blood of His Son and empowered by His most Holy Spirit or they simply won't make any sense.

This book gives simple explanations for each of these topics, referencing Holy Scripture, God's revealed Word and Plan for our salvation, daily life and happiness. There are also many references to the "New" Catechism of the Catholic Church. This "New" Catechism, put out by the Holy See, is a marvelous and necessary book for our Catholic life today. It gives all the basics of our Faith and more. It is the Church's official word on our Faith - which is belief in God's revealed Word to us and our lived response to God's Word and Plan for our lives.

This "New" Catechism should be the primary reference book in every Catholic home next to the family Bible. The

Bible needs to be read and prayed about daily if we are really going to be knowledgeable in living a daily witness to the Gospel of Jesus Christ and His Kingdom. We are the light and hope for the world!

Maria Compton-Hernandez' apologetics book also offers several nice stories and insights as to how parents can explain these various topics to their children at different age levels. It even gives helpful ideas as to how to explain our beliefs to those who are non-Catholic.

If we are to explain what we believe to others, it is important to remember that we must first have a good working knowledge of the core basics of our Faith. We should have a firm understanding of the most Holy Trinity (Father, Son and Holy Spirit), the fall of Adam & Eve and Original Sin, Salvation in the person of Jesus Christ, the commissioned power of the Holy Spirit at Pentecost for the follower of Jesus (our Sacrament of Confirmation), the Seven Sacraments and the ongoing tradition and history of our Church of which we are all a part. We are truly a faith community and not a religion which is simply man's understanding of how he thinks things are or should be.

May God's Holy Spirit give you wisdom, knowledge and insight to know God (Father, Son and Holy Spirit) more clearly and share your faith in a living and dynamic way. With every good blessing and wish on this work I remain your brother in Jesus Christ our Savior.

—Fr. Robert Hilz, T.O.R.
September 14, 1999

# TABLE OF CONTENTS

# INTRODUCTION

When I wrote the book, *The Catholic Mother's Resource Guide*, I thought I had exhausted the topic of ways that parents can teach the Catholic faith to their children. It was after I had been asked to speak publicly to various mothers' groups that the idea that a follow-up work was needed began to germinate. Many parents with whom I met spoke to me about how they wanted to teach the faith well to their kids, but they just didn't know it well enough to do an adequate job. I found lots of questions like, "How can I teach my kids about the Eucharist and the True Presence when I really don't understand it myself?" Some of the most common questions I encountered involved the various doctrines and dogmas of our faith that are much a mystery to today's post Vatican II Catholic: indulgences, purgatory, confession, and many other topics which will be addressed in this work. I hope to address the explanations of such Catholic beliefs primarily in the light of how/why we need to explain them to our children.

The primary purpose of this book is to help mothers and fathers gain a good grasp of the basic doctrines and dogmas of the Roman Catholic faith, in order to be able to explain them more clearly to our children. However, it is likely that all of us will at one time or another be called into question regarding some issue of the Catholic faith by someone who is non-Catholic. Another benefit of learning the very basics of Catholic apologetics is this possibility. It cannot be denied that oftentimes, as Catholic children grow up, they leave the Catholic Faith in order to pursue a Protestant denomination because their parents could not adequately instruct them in what they already had: namely the whole and complete truth in the One, Holy, Catholic, and Apostolic Church. It may safely be said that most who leave the Catholic Church do so in ignorance. How could one leave the actual Presence of Jesus Himself in the Eucharist unless they really did not know and comprehend that and other teachings of our faith? The great Bishop Fulton Sheen once commented that only a handful of people actually hate the Catholic Church, while millions hate what they wrongly perceive the Catholic Church to be.

Many Catholics who are poorly instructed it the Faith are lured away later in life by such things as a fun Protestant church youth group, a friendly and seemingly knowledgeable Jehovah's Witness at their front door, or a 'Bible believing' Protestant colleague at work who brings up misunderstandings about the Catholic faith in a way that appears to be Scripturally sound. As your children grow, you will need to help them achieve a firmer grasp on our precious Catholic faith and all of its beautiful truths to assist in arming them against such ploys which will tear them away from the one, true faith. Throughout this book, I will often refer to our Protestant brethren and what they often misunderstand regarding our faith. For a further explanation on Protestantism and the Reformation, please see the Appendix.

I wish to thank all of the fine apologists who have shared their wealth of knowledge regarding the explanations which will be presented in this work, especially Scott Hahn and Karl Keating, as well as The Catholic Answers staff who have provided such excellent information in their number of Catholic tracts. I hope that this work will serve as a springboard for parents to begin a faith journey to truly enlighten themselves on the rich and wonderful beliefs of our Faith, thus making it easier for them to pass on such beliefs and traditions to our children.

—Maria Compton-Hernandez
September 2, 1999

CHAPTER ONE

# THE IMMACULATE CONCEPTION OF THE BLESSED VIRGIN MARY
## CCC 491-495

As Catholic people, one of the things that makes us truly unique from our Protestant brothers and sisters is our love and honor for the Blessed Mother of Jesus. We believe that Mary, being the Mother of God, deserves the highest respect, devotion, and esteem.

One of the *Dogmas* which the Catholic Church pronounced about her is her Immaculate Conception. This is a Feast Day celebrated on December 8th. There are many Catholics who still misunderstand what this day represents. If you ask a handful of Catholics, "What is the Immaculate Conception?", you will find many will say, "It's that Jesus was conceived in the womb of the Blessed Mother without sin, or without a human father." This is an error that is important to clarify. That is actually known as the Virgin Birth. Yes, of course Jesus was conceived without sin because He was God made man. But the Immaculate Conception is a Dogma which declares that the Blessed Mother was conceived in the womb of her mother, St. Anne, without the stain of original sin. The Blessed Mother is singularly honored by this distinction.

The Blessed Mother was given this preeminence because She was meant to be the pure vessel by which Jesus, the Son of God, would enter into the world. Therefore, She herself had to be preserved from original sin. From the very first instant of Her existence, She was in a state of pure and sanctifying grace - literally "full of grace." We use these words when we refer to her in the Hail Mary, but many don't take the time to reflect on what these words really mean.

When the angel Gabriel appeared to the Blessed Mother during the Annunciation, he was the one who first used this important title:

> Hail, full of grace, the Lord is with you.
> —Luke 1:28

This phrase 'full of grace' when translated from the Greek text, is actually used as a direct reference to Mary. The Greek term used illustrates that She was in a state of complete, or perfected grace from the moment of Her conception throughout Her earthly life.

Does it not make perfect sense that God would want a pure vessel that was spotless from all stain of sin to carry the His Only Begotten Son? After all, Jesus, while in the womb of Mary, grew and developed in the way that all babies do within their mothers. He actually shared Her blood and was nourished through His growth from Mary's very body.

Some fundamentalists object to this dogma by saying that Mary spoke of her "spirit rejoicing in God my Savior." Why would she need a savior, they ask, if she was without sin? The Church teaches that because she was descended from Adam, by Her very nature she would normally have contracted original sin. It was by a singular and unique intervention on God's behalf that she was spared this. So, she was indeed redeemed by Christ's grace, but in a very special way. The grace was poured upon Her before she was conceived in her parent's womb.

Fundamentalists also will say that this dogma is refuted because Scripture says in Romans 3:23 that "all have sinned." However, if we clearly look at this we can see there are some exceptions to this. Consider a child below the age of reason. We do not believe that such a young child can sin, because sinning requires the ability to reason and an intent to sin.

If such a young child dies before the age of reason, he has not yet sinned. The Scripture passage "all have sinned" would not apply to this child. Therefore, we can see this was an exception to this scripture passage. Scripture also teaches that even though all have sinned, Jesus was true man and did not sin. It is logical to further state that Mary did not sin either, and was preserved from even original sin so that she could remain the constant pure repository to carry the Christ child.

In teaching about the Immaculate Conception Dogma to our children, the primary focus should be making sure they have a grasp on the basic teaching and what it means. Explain it in simple terms or analogies that the child can relate to:

> You know that Adam and Eve were the first people that God created. God gave them everything they could ever want in Paradise, the Garden of Eden. But He told them not to eat of a certain tree. Lucifer, the fallen angel, came to them and tempted them to eat the fruit from this tree. When Adam and Eve ate this fruit, they disobeyed God and were thrown out of Paradise. Because of this first sin, all people born since Adam and Eve have what's called "original sin". That's why when a baby is born, they are baptized soon after birth so that they can have this original sin removed from their soul and become pure and clean, a child of God.

When God needed to send His Son, Jesus, into the world to save us, He also needed a pure woman to carry Jesus in Her womb. God decided that this woman should not have the original sin of Adam and Eve. He decided that this woman would be special and must be very clean and pure.

It's kind of like if you have a pitcher of fresh lemonade, you wouldn't pour it into an old, dirty bucket to drink it, would you? You would pour the lemonade into nice, clean glasses to drink. So God didn't want His only Son to grow in the womb of a woman who had sin. That's why God made Mary be free from all sin when She was made in the womb of her mother, St. Anne. This is called the Immaculate Conception - those are big words, but they mean that Mary did not have the original sin of Adam and Eve so that She could be a pure mother to carry Jesus in Her womb.

Simple explanations can do wonders to clarify from the very beginning what the main dogmas and doctrines of our faith teach us. Let's move on to the another Dogma of the Blessed Mother.

## PRAYER TO OUR
## IMMACULATE MOTHER MARY

*Lord God, You prepared a worthy dwelling place for Your Son by the Immaculate Conception of the Virgin, grant we pray, that as You preserved her from all stain of sin in Your foreknowledge of his death, so we, by her intercession, may come to You with pure hearts. We ask this through Christ our Lord. Amen.*

CHAPTER TWO

# THE PERPETUAL
# VIRGINITY OF MARY
### CCC. 496-511

Since we are on the various doctrines related to the Blessed Mother,we will now discuss another belief that Catholics hold dear: that Mary remained a Virgin Her entire life and never had any more children after Jesus. Jesus was conceived by the power of the Holy Spirit within the pure and sinless womb of the Virgin Mary. Unlike our separated brethern, we also believe that She remained a virgin throughout Her earthly life. Most Protestants contend that She had more children after Jesus. The confusion about this issue comes as a result of about ten instances in the New Testament in which the terms "brothers" and "sisters" of the Lord are used (Matt. 13:55, Mark 3:31-34, Luke 8:19-20 are a few). Your own children may ask you about his after hearing some of these verses read in Mass, so it's important to know how to explain this concept.

In these Scripture passages, the terms "brother and sister" are translated from the Greek words *adelphos*, *adelphe* or *adelphoi*. The Greek forms of these words often refers to cousins or kinsman: those who are members of the family by marriage or law, though not directly related. The reason for the confusion is that the Hebrew and Aramaic languages spoken by Christ and His disciples did not have a special word to denote cousin or kinsman, so the word 'brother' or 'sister' was used instead. This is a great little tidbit of information to have stored away in case a questioning Protestant insists that Jesus had earthly brothers and sisters based on these Scripture passages.

One of the key documents that helps us to also prove Mary's perpetual virginity is a document called the "Protoevangelium of James." This document was written no later than 120 A.D., less than 60 years after the conclusion of Mary's earthly life.

The entire document is a testament to the fact that Mary remained ever virgin. It's also interesting to note, especially when discussing this concept with Protestants, that the Protestant reformers like Martin Luther and John Calvin honored the teaching of the perpetual virginity of Mary as the authentic teaching of the Bible, even though, ironically, most modern day Protestants do not. If your children ask what the passages referring to the 'brothers and sisters' of Jesus mean, it's adequate to say that they simply refer to Jesus' cousins. Some of the apostles were blood cousins of Jesus, including St. Jude and St. James. A final proof for the fact that Jesus had no other blood brothers or sisters is apparent in the passage of Scripture which refers to the crucifixion:

> Standing by the cross of Jesus were his mother and his mother's sister, Mary the wife of Clopas, and Mary of Magdala. When Jesus saw his mother and the disciple there whom he loved, he said to his mother, "Woman, behold your son." Then he said to the disciple, 'Behold your mother.' And from that hour the disciple took her into his home.
> —John 19: 25-28

If Jesus actually had other earthly brothers and sisters, it would have been customary by Jewish law that he bequeath her care to them. Instead he chooses St. John the Apostle, who was not related to Him by blood. This is a clear proof that Jesus had no other brothers and sisters, or else he would have followed Jewish custom and asked them to care for their mother after his death.

As parents, we can take great comfort in the fact that the virtue of chastity was of utmost importance to Our Lady. St. Joseph also respected and lived by this virtue of chastity during his life with the Blessed Mother. In prayer, he is sometimes invoked as the "Virgin Father" of Jesus, as well as the foster father. They lived in holy and platonic love, as brother and sister. Both St. Joseph and Our Lady are wonderful examples of purity and chastity that mothers and fathers should pray to often for intercession, especially as our children grow into their teenage years and may have numerous temptations against their own chastity.

> How would we have acted, if we could have chosen our own mother? I'm sure we would have chosen the one we have, adorning her with every possible grace. That is what Christ did. Christ being all-powerful, all-wise, Love itself, His power carried out His Will.... This is the clearest reason why our Lord granted his mother, from the very moment of her Immaculate Conception, all possible privileges. She was free from the power of Satan. She is beautiful, spotless, and pure in soul and body.
>
> —Blessed Josemaria Escriva
> "Christ is Passing By You", Princeton, NJ, Scepter Pub, 1968.

# CHAPTER THREE

# THE ASSUMPTION OF THE BLESSED MOTHER INTO HEAVEN
### CCC. 966, 974

The dogma of the Blessed Mother known as the Assumption celebrates the truth that after Her earthly life, Mary was assumed (taken up) body and soul into Heaven. In Scripture, Gen.5:24 and 2 Chron. 2:1-13 describe the bodies of the prophets Enoch and Elijah as being taken up into Heaven, so it was not an event that was unprecedented. The Church has never formally defined whether the Blessed Mother actually died, though most scholars agree that she did. Recently Pope John Paul II reflected in a weekly meditation that "the mother is not superior to the Son," and reinforced the belief that Mary experienced an earthly death. Since Jesus Himself had to die, it would be logical to assume that the Blessed Mother had to physically die before Her Assumption as well.

Since we believe that the Blessed Mother was conceived without sin and remained 'full of grace' throughout Her earthly life, it is also logical to infer that Her body would not have to undergo corruption on earth after death. Perhaps the greatest proof we have of the Assumption of the Blessed Virgin is what might be called 'negative proof.' If Mary had been buried somewhere in the world, there would most definitely be a tomb. The Blessed Mother was greatly respected and loved by the early Church. The early Church members jealously guarded relics, remains, and earthly belongings from the martyrs of the Church. We know the spot of the birth of Jesus, the place of the Crucifixion, the location of the Ascension of Christ, and many other prominent places which relate to the life of Christ.

We know because our early Church brethren passed on this information to us through Sacred Tradition. Relics of the earliest members of the Church, the Twelve Apostles, are still in existence, and there are also relics of Christ like the Shroud of Turin and actual pieces of the True Cross.

It would be most logical to presume that if the Blessed Mother had an earthly tomb, it would have been highly revered and honored by the early Church. She was, after all, the Mother of God. None of the cities that the Blessed Mother lived in, namely Ephesus nor Jerusalem, claim to have the tomb of Mary. Why would no city lay claim to Her remains? Because there simply are none to be found on earth.

Once again, if you ever have occasion to discuss the Assumption with fundamentalists, you will find they disagree with this dogma. Conversely, though, many fundamentalists believe that some day we will all be 'raised up' and raptured (caught up and taken into Heaven) by referring to the Scripture passage: 1 Thess. 4: 17. We believe that Mary was simply given this privilege early. And why shouldn't She be given such a gift to have Her body preserved from earthly corruption? We can clearly see how the dogmas of the Immaculate Conception and the Assumption go hand in hand. When explaining the Assumption to your children, it's a great time to reiterate the Immaculate Conception:

> Remember when we celebrated the Immaculate Conception? We believe that God made Mary within the womb of her

mother, St. Anne, without any sin. He made Her this way so that she could carry Jesus, who is God. At the end of the Blessed Mother's life on earth, God decided to do something very special for Her. Instead of having her body be buried somewhere, He just raised Her body right into Heaven. This is called the Assumption. The Blessed Mother was taken up with her earthly body along with Her soul right into Heaven so She could be with Jesus. This was a very special thing that God did for Mary because He loves Her so much. Now Mary is the Queen of Heaven and Earth.

If you ever get into discussions with fundamentalists and other Protestants who refer to themselves as "Bible-believing Christians," you will discover a fundamental flaw in their arguments. Most of these fundamentalists will reject the doctrines of the Immaculate Conception, the Assumption, Purgatory, and a host of other Catholic beliefs, by using the simple argument that you can't find those words or references in the Bible, therefore, it didn't happen. This belief that everything must be found verbatim in Scripture is called *Sola Scriptura*. It literally means "Scripture alone" - the Bible only. The flaw with the 'sola scriptura' theory is that, ironically, you cannot find the words 'sola scriptura', 'Scripture only', 'the Bible only', etc. in Scripture either! While Scripture clearly teaches us its importance, there are many references to Sacred Tradition, and the fact that there are many more things which were never recorded in Scripture: (CCC 80-83)

> Many other signs also did Jesus in the sight of his disciples, which are not written in this book.
> —John 20: 30

> Therefore, brethren, stand fast; and hold the
> traditions which you have learned, whether by
> word, or by our epistle.
>
> —2 Thess. 20:14

The power for the Church to define the dogmas of
the Immaculate Conception and the Assumption comes
from the teaching authority which Jesus gave to Peter and the
early Church. The fact that these words and events are not
specifically mentioned in Scripture does not mean they did not
happen. The Church defined them clearly and explicitly for the
faithful because Jesus promised us He would infallibly guide
and teach His Church through the leadership and magisterium
until the end of time.

Another reason many Protestants have a hard time
finding biblical support for many Catholic doctrines is because
their version of the Bible, based on the King James Version,
is still missing several key books. Therefore, their Bible is
incomplete. For a further explanation of this, see the Appendix
on the Protestant Reformation. The Sacred Tradition which
gives us the doctrines of the Immaculate Conception and the
Assumption is actually older than the New Testament books of
the Bible, which did not appear until around 350-400 A.D.

> Mary has gone to heaven in both body and
> soul, and the angels rejoice. I can imagine,
> too, the delight of St. Joseph, her most chaste
> spouse, who awaited her in paradise. Yet what
> of us who remain on earth? Our faith tells
> us that here below, in our present life, we are
> pilgrims wayfarers. Our lot is one of suffering, of
> sacrifices, and privations. Nonetheless, joy must
> mark the rhythm of our steps. 'Serve the Lord
> with joy' - there is no other way to serve him.
> —Blessed Josemaria Escriva from
> "Christ is Passing By You," Princeton, NJ, Scepter Pub, 1968.

CHAPTER FOUR

# THE EXISTENCE OF PURGATORY
## CCC 1030-1032

The belief in the existence of Purgatory is a fundamental Catholic truth which shows how incredibly merciful our God truly is. The *Catechism of the Catholic Church* defines it like this:

> All who die in God's grace and friendship, but still imperfectly purified, are indeed assured of their eternal salvation; but after death they undergo purification, so as to achieve the holiness necessary to enter the joy of heaven. The Church gives the name Purgatory to this final purification of the elect, which is entirely different from the punishment of the damned.
> (CCC 1030-1)

It is a most wonderful sign of the mercy of God that there is another option after death aside from heaven and hell. Let's look at the Scripture references which support the belief in Purgatory:

> It is therefore a holy and wholesome thought to pray for the dead, that they may be loosed from their sins.
> —2 Macc. 12: 43-46

Now, if our options were only heaven and hell, there would be no need of prayers by the faithful after we have departed. One in heaven is not in need of prayers, and one in hell is there for eternity and no prayers could assist him either. So the idea of a place of purification before entering heaven goes back to the Old Testament. In fact, Eastern Orthodox and Jews have always historically upheld the belief in such a place of purification. It was not until the Protestant Reformation in the 1500's that anyone denied this fundamental truth.

The New Testament also has a variety of references to a place of purification after death:

> Every man's work shall be manifest; for the Day of the Lord shall declare it, because it shall be revealed in fire; and the fire shall try every man's work, of what sort it is. ... If any man's work burn, he shall suffer loss; but he himself shall be saved, as yet by fire.
> —1 Cor. 3: 13-14

In this verse, the "Day" refers to the great day of judgment when each individual will personally be called to accept responsibility for their lifetime's actions. The reference to fire as purification for works that were not yet perfect also illustrate the place of Purgatory, as a place for us to be purified before entering into heaven.

We see Jesus refer to this place of purification in another reference:

> And whoever speaks a word against the Son of Man will be forgiven; but whoever speaks against the Holy Spirit will not be forgiven, either in this age or in the age to come.
> —Matt 12:32

How does this refer to Purgatory? Jesus is referring to sins which can be forgiven in the age to come (after death). If one goes to heaven, they cannot have the sins forgiven there. If an individual goes to hell, their sins cannot be forgiven there, either. There must be a place where certain types of sin which are not against the Holy Spirit can be forgiven. These references to Purgatory are subtle and sometimes it takes a good study Bible with extensive footnotes to fully understand them.

Jesus refers to a place of purgation again in this passage:

> If you are to go with your opponent before the magistrate, make an effort to settle the matter on the way; otherwise your opponent will turn you over to the judge, and the judge hand you over to the constable, and the constable throw you into prison. I say to you, you will not be released until you have paid the last penny.
> —Luke 12: 58-59

In this sort of parable, Jesus does not mention Purgatory by name. But he again alludes to it by saying "You will not be released until you have paid the last penny." Jesus is referring to the judgment day in this allegory. Here He insinuates that some payment may need to be made before the judgment will be complete. In Purgatory, one must stay until he has fully satisfied the punishment due to his earthly sins - "not until he has paid the last penny" will he be released and allowed to enter into heaven.

The Church teaches us that the Holy Souls in Purgatory are officially known as the *Church Suffering* because they are undergoing purification before entering into Heaven. There may be said to be a sort of joy in Purgatory, though, despite the suffering. This joy is because the Poor Souls in Purgatory are assured of their salvation. They have made it to Purgatory, so they cannot be damned to Hell. They are confident that after their stay in Purgatory, they will be permitted to enter into everlasting bliss in Heaven and will never have to undergo the permanent fires of Hell. The second branch of the Church after the *Church Suffering* is the *Church Militant*. We who still are working out our daily salvation are considered to be members of this group. The third branch is *Church Triumphant*, the full company of the Communion of Saints in heaven.

These three branches of the Church are intermingled—we pray and work together to form the Body of Christ. This means that the Poor Souls in Purgatory can pray for us on earth, and we can and should do the same for them. The Poor Souls are waiting for our prayers on their behalf, as they cannot pray for themselves. That is why developing an awareness of Purgatory in your children and a devotion of praying on their behalf is so important.

So now we have the Scriptural references to help us see the doctrine of Purgatory. How can we parents explain this thought to our children in a way they will understand? I found the best way to teach such doctrines is through allegories that children can easily comprehend.

Here's the one I use to describe why we have Purgatory:

> Imagine this: you were invited to attend a grand ball, a wonderful party, and everyone there was wearing their finest clothes, had their hair done up beautifully, had been bathed and were clean and sweet-smelling.

The host of the party answers the door and you are invited to enter. But you are standing there in horrible rags. Your hair is tangled and smelly, and you are unclean and need a bath. Would you want to enter into that party?

When I proposed this scene to my questioning five year old, she stated, "Oh no, Mom! I'd want to go get cleaned up and get some nice clothes on first!" That's when I explained that this is what Purgatory is for: to 'get cleaned up' - our souls, that is - to cleanse us of our sins and the punishment due to those sins before we enter into the perfect beauty of heaven.

My seven-year-old came up with her own analogy when asked to explain Purgatory to her class: she said it's kind of like a doctor's office waiting room. This has some truth to it, in the fact that it is a time of waiting. But the waiting that the Poor Souls must undergo is likely much more painful than the annoying waiting of a doctor's office!

Here are some practices you may wish to establish with your kids to develop a devotion of praying for the Poor Souls.

1) Say a quick prayer when passing a graveyard. The standard prayer has always been:

   Eternal rest grant unto them, O Lord, and let perpetual light shine upon them, may they rest in peace.

   If you recite this prayer aloud enough times each time you pass by a graveyard, they will eventually learn it. But for very young children, shorten it until they are capable of learning the entire prayer to "God rest their souls."

2) Teach children the value of praying for anyone they know who has recently died.

This would include people they read about or hear about in the news, regardless of if they personally knew them. The point is that we don't really know if that soul went to Purgatory first, but we offer prayers on their behalf *in case* they did. God in his infinite wisdom can take these prayers and apply them to other needy souls in Purgatory if that particular soul did not go to Purgatory.

3) Sprinkle a few drops of holy water on behalf of the Poor Souls when you pass by a holy water font.

Say this prayer or one of your own:

Dear Lord, by the power of this holy water and your Precious Blood, please multiply these drops of water to provide relief for the Poor Souls in Purgatory.

4) Help your children learn to make acts of mortification on behalf of the Poor Souls.

One way is to 'offer up' the pain of a stubbed toe, knocked funny bone, etc. to Jesus especially for the Poor Souls. This doesn't make the pain go away, but offering up the pain with something as simple as "Jesus I give you this pain as an offering for the Poor Souls in Purgatory. Amen!" is a very efficacious practice. We will not know until we get to heaven how many Poor Souls we were able to help enter into Heaven by such practices. These souls who go to heaven as a result of our prayers and mortifications will be very dear to us and remember us in a special way in their prayers after they have joined in the communion of saints.

Unfortunately, today many Catholic schools fail miserably to teach our children about the reality of Purgatory. In many schools it is not even mentioned. It is one of the mainstays of the faith that has simply been swept under the rug in religious instruction.

This is a grave error for the coming generations - who is praying for the Poor Souls in Purgatory? Who will be left to pray for us if, by God's grace, we are able to make it to Purgatory after our death? Once again, it is up to us as Catholic parents to insure that our kids have an understanding of this belief and develop a devotion of interceding for the Poor Souls.

## A Prayer For The Poor Souls

*O Holy Souls, which have passed from this world into Purgatory, and who are awaited eagerly in Heaven, pray for me and ask for all the graces I need, and for which I beg the Divine Majesty. Amen.*

(Source: Taken from the book "Devotion for Poor Souls," Warsaw, Jan. 1903)

CHAPTER FIVE

# THE REALITY OF HELL
CCC. 1033 - 1037

In both Catholic and Protestant churches today there exists a new and dangerous theological concept: there is no hell, because a God of mercy would never damn one of His chosen creatures to eternal fire. You will find there are very few religious ed classes, CCD classes, and religion classes in Catholic schools that even mention the reality of hell to children anymore. The danger of such liberal theology is that we are raising a generation of children who have lost a belief in the reality of hell. As a result, they are not fearful of their own sinful actions. After all, if there is no place of punishment, why should one worry about the consequences of sin?

As Catholic parents, we must instill a healthy fear and realization of the doctrine of hell. It is not a point that should be obsessed upon, but certainly one of which children must be made aware. First, let's look at some of the many Scriptural references to hell:

> ...It is better for thee to enter lame into life everlasting than having two feet, to be cast into the hell of unquenchable fire: Where the worm dies not, and the fire is not extinguished...
> —Mark 9: 42-47

...Then he will say to you, I do not know
where you are from. Depart from me, all you
evildoers!' And there will be wailing and
grinding of teeth when you see Abraham,
Isaac, and Jacob and all the prophets in the
kingdom of God and you yourselves cast out.
—Luke 13: 27-28

Then he will say to those on his left, Depart
from me, you accursed, into the eternal fire
prepared for the devil and his angels.
—Matt. 25:41

The whole problem with the "God is love and mercy
only" theology, which insists there cannot be a place like
Hell, is that it is fundamentally flawed. Those who hold such
a belief do so because they believe God is *only* a God of mercy
and love - they deny that He is also a God of *justice*. Let's
look at some Scriptural references to illustrate that our God
is a God of justice, as well as mercy, love and forgiveness:

For his eyes are upon the ways of man, and he
beholds all his steps. There is no darkness so
dense that evildoers can hide in it. Therefore
he discerns their works; he turns at night and
crushes them... Because they turned away
from him and heeded none of his ways, but
caused the cries of the poor to reach him, so
that he heard the plea of the afflicted. If he
remains tranquil, who then can condemn? If
he hides his face, who then can behold him?
—Job 34: 21-29

For he doth wrong, shall receive for that
which he hath done wrongfully; and there is

no respect of persons with God.'
—Col. 3:25

And if the just man shall scarcely be saved,
where shall the ungodly and the sinner
appear?
—1 Peter 4: 18

And so we clearly see that while our God is certainly
one of mercy and love, He is also a God of justice and equity.
We will all be called into a fair and just accounting of our life
when we die and stand before the throne of the Almighty.
God gives each person a lifetime of opportunities in which
we will decide whether or not we will serve Him. At the end
of it all, it is the individual soul who *chooses to go to hell* if he
has lived a lifetime of rejecting God. To say that God condemns a soul to Hell is fundamentally inaccurate.

That soul has *chosen* to go to hell by their lifetime's
actions and rejection of God, even at that final moment of
judgment. That soul also chooses to ignore the mercy of
God and, through pride, chooses to continue the denial and
rejection of God, even at the final moment of judgment.

As parents, present the reality of the consequences of
sin to your children. The options after death are three: heaven,
hell and purgatory. Explain Hell in terms that are simple, yet
will have an impact. I use the Scriptural description of Hell,
because I don't believe Jesus was speaking figuratively. Hell is,
quite literally, a place of unending pain and torture. But the
greatest pain is the total and never-ending absence of God.
This is not a cruel or frightening thought and it is certainly
not too much for children to bear. It's quite believable that
someone who lives a life of sin and rejection of God, would
choose to reject and turn his back on God at the final moment

and live in eternal fire without Him.

When we see examples of sin in our society, like abortion, which certainly call down the wrath of God upon those who support it, we must explain to the children that this is an example of something which would lead one to an eternity in Hell. However, we don't pass judgment on particular law makers or individuals who support such practices, we simply say that if their hearts don't change that they may likely end up in Hell for their practices.

We can further explain the outrages and truly evil horrors which are occurring in our world today by the reality of the devil. He was an angel of light for the Lord and his name, "Lucifer," means 'angel of light.' Lucifer decided he did not wish to serve our Lord and was cast out of Heaven with many other fallen angels. They now reign in Hell, and work hard at robbing souls from God by tempting them to sin.

The many horrors of our society like abortion, contraception, divorce, violence, promiscuity and various aberrant sexual behaviors which gravely offend our Lord, are all a direct result of man's turning away from God. These issues should also be discussed with our children if the opportunity presents itself. We became involved in extensive discussions with our older children (ages 8, 7, 5) when the 1996 elections were in full swing. The issue of abortion was a primary one, and it was necessary for us to explain to them what this practice involved and why certain candidates would be unacceptable. Of course, the depth of the information you impart to your children involving such issues will depend on their age and maturity level.

# CHAPTER SIX

# THE CORNERSTONE OF IT ALL... THE EUCHARIST
## CCC. 1362-1405

The Eucharist is the source and summit of what being a Roman Catholic is all about. As Catholic people, we believe that at the moment of Consecration during the Mass, when the priest repeats the words Jesus Himself said at the Last Supper, "This is my Body... This is my Blood..." a miracle occurs. The bread and wine which the priest consecrates actually becomes the Body, Blood, Soul and Divinity of Jesus Christ. Our non-Catholic brothers and sisters insist that the bread and wine are mere symbols of our Lord, but as Catholics we know that is not the case.

How can we be so sure that this consecrated bread and wine, the Eucharist, is truly our Lord and not merely symbolic? Let's turn to Scripture first, where Jesus Himself makes it abundantly clear that He was not speaking symbolically, nor metaphorically. In John 6 we read that Jesus had just finished performing the miracle of the multiplication of the loaves. As the chapter progresses, Jesus says the words which are known as "the Bread of Life Discourse."

> "Amen, amen, I say to you, it was not Moses who gave you bread from Heaven; my Father gives you the true bread of heaven. For the bread of God is that which comes down from

heaven and gives life to the world." So they said to him, "Sir, give us this bread always." Jesus said to them, "I am the bread of life; whoever comes to me will never hunger, and whoever believes in me will never thirst.

—John 6: 32-36

I am the bread of life. Your ancestors ate the manna in the desert, but they died; this is the bread that comes down from heaven so that one may eat it and not die. I am the living bread that came down from Heaven; whoever eats this bread will live forever; and the bread that I will give is my flesh for the life of the world.

—John 6: 48-51

After Jesus spoke these words so emphatically, Scripture tells us that the Jewish people were scandalized at what he was suggesting. Jesus could see their scandal, and he proceeded to reiterate this belief even further:

Amen, amen, I say to you, unless you eat the flesh of the Son of Man and drink his Blood, you do not have life in you. Whoever eats my Flesh and drinks my Blood has eternal life, and I will raise him on the last day. For my Flesh is true food and my Blood is true drink. Whoever eats my Flesh and drinks my Blood remains in me and I in him.

—John 6: 53 - 57

Jesus is speaking directly to the Jews who have just been scandalized by the thought that they were expected to actually eat his flesh and drink his blood. Now if he meant that this was only a metaphor, or that he was just speaking symbolically, don't you think he would have rephrased things a bit to clarify with the Jews that they were misunderstanding him? In fact, many of the disciples present said that it was a hard teaching and they could not accept it. A large number of them turned and walked away that day then and there..

> ...As a result of this, many of his disciples drew
> back and no longer went about with him.'
> —John 6:66

If our Lord could see that his words were causing them to leave him as a result of a simple misunderstanding, surely he would have stopped them and said,

> Hey! Wait a minute! No, I didn't mean *you
> actually have to eat my flesh and drink my blood*!
> I was speaking symbolically! Come back!"

But our Lord did not stop them from leaving, simply because those that walked away understood Him perfectly. He spoke accurately and truly when he said that His flesh and blood needed to be consumed by us, and that was what they had trouble accepting.

To further this in Scripture, St. Paul says:

> Therefore, whoever eats the bread or drinks
> the cup of the Lord unworthily will have to
> answer for the body and blood of the Lord.
> —1 Cor 11: 27-30

St. Paul is clearly indicating that he believes the consecrated bread and wine to be the actual Body and Blood of the Lord, otherwise why would he insist that partaking in the Eucharist unworthily or in a state of sin would bring one condemnation? If the Eucharist was merely a symbol, that is, just a piece of bread, then partaking of it unworthily would not be scandalous or damning. Just as tearing up a picture of someone (which is symbolic of them, represents them) is not a sinful act in itself. But, if you instead cause bodily harm to that person directly, that is sinful and brings condemnation. Thus, St. Paul clearly states that if you eat and drink of the Flesh and Blood of our Lord unworthily, you are bringing damnation upon yourself. Clearly he states this because he holds to the belief that the Eucharist is the True Presence of Jesus among us.

We can foster this belief in the True Presence with our children by being careful with how we choose our words. Refer to the Eucharist as "The Eucharist" or "The Body of Jesus" - not "the host" alone, unless you are providing further explanation. Likewise, refer to the Blood of our Lord as "The Precious Blood" as opposed to "the wine" after it has been consecrated.

When speaking to very little ones, it suffices to say as you prepare to go up to receive Holy Communion, "I'm going to go receive Jesus now." Bring your children with you to be blessed by the priest and to witness your reception of the Eucharist.

Another way to foster belief and understanding of the True Presence with our children is by occasional visits to see the "Hidden Jesus" in the tabernacle, or to see our Lord's exposition in the Blessed Sacrament, or during Eucharistic Adoration (when the faithful may worship in Jesus' Eucharistic Presence) exposed for public adoration. Even little ones can do short visits of 2 - 3 minutes. Older children, ages 6 - 9 or so can do longer visits with time of

15-20 minutes or longer, depending on your child. One time I brought my 3 oldest (ages 9,7, and 6) to share a Holy Hour as a family. Each of us took 15 minute shifts with Jesus, while the others played on the nearby school playground. I was pleasantly surprised to see that even my often-distracted 6 year old could pull her own 15 minute shift without too much trouble. Simple acts such as saying *'Say good-bye to Jesus!'* to a little one upon leaving after a visit help to make it a point to even little ones that it is really Jesus there. Help make it a point with even the little ones that Jesus is really there by saying, "*Goodbye Jesus!*" as you conclude your visit.

One night when I was at Eucharistic Adoration with my seven year old, a man entered the chapel to use as a 'walk through' and zipped out the side door without even acknowledging our Lord present in the monstrance at all. Later, I was surprised to hear my daughter comment about how wrong it was for him not to acknowledge Jesus in the monstrance. She said, "Gosh, mom, if Jesus was sitting there with his Body on a throne, that guy would never have done that!" The simple things we do to help our children understand this cornerstone of our faith, just the words we choose and actions we display will help them grasp this concept that even some learned theologians cannot comprehend.

We also need to distinguish with our children that not all Churches are Catholic, thus those that are not do not have the True Presence of Jesus in the Eucharist.

While some churches have 'communion celebrations,' the bread and wine that is distributed is simply that: bread and wine. It has not been consecrated by an ordained Catholic priest, so it is not called "the Eucharist" or *true* "Holy Communion." If your child is ever invited to attend a Protestant service in which a type of 'communion' will be passed out, please make it clear that they are not to take part in such a meal. Also, be sure if your child has a friend who is non-Catholic attend a Catholic Mass, that the friend is not to receive the Holy Eucharist. Explain that it is because you cannot receive the Eucharist unless you are a Catholic and have had instruction in the teaching that the Eucharist really is our Lord. It would be wrong for someone who believes that the Eucharist is not really our Lord to receive Him.

When you drive by Catholic Churches, make the Sign of the Cross and perhaps say a short prayer out loud to reinforce the fact that Jesus is really present there in the tabernacle. Make it a point to explain why we don't do this when driving by Protestant churches - because Jesus in not present there in the bodily sense as He is in Catholic Churches in the Eucharist. And, of course, when you enter or leave a Catholic Church, be sure to genuflect towards the tabernacle to show respect for our Lord's True Presence.

In the back of the resource section you will find two areas you may wish to explore. The first are prayers to say before receiving the Eucharist. One of the prayers is a prayer for expectant mothers to say before receiving Holy Communion. What a powerful and reassuring thought: to be able to know that the Eucharist will not only nourish us when we receive it, but also it will actually nourish the child that grows within us. Another section is a pull out that you may wish to cut out and staple, laminate, or bind to have for your young child (ages preschool to about 4th grade). The section can be read by you to your child, or your child may read it as a reflection on Our Eucharistic Lord while in adoration or as preparation for making First Holy Communion.

# CHAPTER SEVEN

# CONFESSION
CCC. 1440-1470

Perhaps one of the most misundrstood sacraments in the Catholic Church is Confession or Reconciliation. It is not only gravely misunderstood by Protestants, but by many Catholics as well. This is confirmed by the fact that only a small percentage of practicing Catholics follow the Church's instruction to attend Confession at least once a year. We are expressly told by St. Paul that when we do not go to Confession to cleanse us of serious sin before receiving Holy Communion, we are guilty of profaning the Body and Blood of the Lord (1 Cor. 11: 27). There are a number of Scriptural references which refer to the Sacrament of Confession:

> If we confess our sins, he is faithful and just, and will forgive our sins and cleanse us from all unrighteousness.
> —1 John 1: 19

The Church teaches us that we especially need Confession for grave or mortal sins which are a danger to our eternal salvation. However, frequent confession as a means of tremendous grace, even for venial sins, is a practice the Church also recommends. The approved devotions of First Friday/First Saturday recommend monthly Confession, regardless of the presence of mortal sin. It is said that the Pope himself takes advantage of daily Confession! Clearly,

Jesus imparted the mission to forgive sins in His name when He commissioned his apostles:

> As the Father has sent me, even so I send you....
> Receive the Holy Spirit. If you forgive the sins
> of any, they are forgiven; if you retain the sins
> of any, they are retained.
>
> —John 20: 21

If Jesus was not imparting the sacred duty of Confession to His first priests and bishops here, what exactly was He saying? Protestants argue that they can go 'straight to God' to have their sins forgiven. Of course, it would be impossible to confess every venial sin we commit, but the Sacrament of Confession is required for mortal sins, or Christ would not have instituted it here so clearly in this passage. We are also encouraged to express our daily faults and failings directly to God, but the actual act of forgiveness of grave sins must occur during a sacramental Confession.

We see the priest who gives us absolution as the representative of Jesus Himself. Even though we are 'confessing' our sins directly to this man who is the priest, it is Jesus Himself who give us the forgiveness. Jesus gives this power of absolution to the ordained vocation of the priest. If your child complains that he doesn't like to go to Confession to Fr. So and So, explain that it is really *Jesus* who gives us the forgiveness. Jesus is there in the person of the ordained priest to offer us this forgiveness. Our personal feelings towards that particular priest are really not a factor. The reality is that we still receive the forgiveness for our sins in the name of Jesus and His Church regardless of which priest is sitting there hearing the Confession. That priest is a human person who sins, but he is nonetheless given the authority and duty to offer us forgiveness *in the name of Jesus* by the power he received through his priestly ordination.

Try to make it a practice within your home to go to frequent Confession. When your child becomes old enough to partake in this wonderful grace-filled Sacrament, monthly Confession is a great practice to start. Some complaints I hear regarding going to frequent Confession are, "I just don't feel anything. I don't get anything out of it. I just confess the same thing every month...I don't feel like I've sinned in the last month since I confessed...etc..." No, we don't always "feel something" when we go to Confession, especially if we go monthly. We do not usually have grave sins to confess,but usually sins of omission and daily faults and weaknesses.

*Sins of omissions* are those actions which would have been good or benefited the Kingdom of God in one way or another, but which we daily neglect to do. Surely all of us have these types of sin we can confess! We don't need to feel anything to receive the wonderful graces of the Sacrament of Reconciliation. But these graces nevertheless fortify us monthly to avoid other sins and to overcome our weaknesses. If you begin the practice of monthly Confession starting at the earliest possible age, it may become a lifelong habit to empower your children with the ability to avoid serious sin through their teenage and adult life. We mothers and fathers must be the example when it comes to this practice of monthly Confession. Make it a family duty to do this together.

## THE TEN COMMANDMENTS
### (Examination of Conscience)

I. I am the Lord Your God, You shall not have strange gods before me.

Have I performed my duties toward God grudgingly or reluctantly? Did I neglect my prayer life? Did I receive Holy Communion always in a state of grace? Did I ever violate the one-hour Eucharisitic Fast? Did I ever fail to mention known grave sins in Confession?

II.  You Shall not take the name of the Lord Thy God in Vain.

Did I make use of God's name mockingly, jokingly, angrily, or in any irreverent manner? Did I make use of the name of the Blessed Virgin Mary or any other saint's name in an irreverent manner? Did I tell a lie under oath? Did I break private (or public) vows?

III.  Remember to Keep Holy the Sabbath.

Did I miss Mass on Sunday or a Holy Day of Obligation? Did I fail to dress myself and my family appropriately and reverently for Sunday Mass? Did I arrive late to Mass or leave early without sufficient reason? Did I cause others to be distracted? Did I fail to generously support the church financially?

IV.  Honor your Father and Mother.

Have I neglected to teach my children their prayers, send them to Church or give them a Christian education? Have I given them a bad example? Have I neglected to watch over my children, to monitor their companions, the books they read, the movies and t.v. shows they watch?

V.  You Shall not Kill.

Did I easily get angry or lose my temper? Was I envious or jealous of others? Did I injure or take the life of another? Was I reckless in driving? Did I get drunk or use prohibited drugs? Have I lead others into sin? Did I neglect my own health? Did I cause harm to anyone with my words or actions?

VI. You Shall not Commit Adultery.
IX. You Shall not covet your neighbor's wife.

Did I willfully entertain impure thoughts? Did I consent to eveil desires against the virtue of purity, even though I may not have carried them out? Did I engage in imPure conversations or jokes? Did I fail to take care of details of modesty and purity for myself and my children? Did I lead others to sins of impurity or immodesty? Did I use contraception or have myself or my husband sterilized?

VII.   You Shall not Steal.

X.   You Shall not covet your neighbor's goods.

Have I caused damage to another's property? Did I harm anyone by deception, fraud or coercion in business contracts or transactions? Do I give alms according to my capability? Did I neglect to pay my debts? Did I knowingly accept stolen goods? Did I desire to steal? Was I greedy?

VIII.   You Shall not Bear False Witness.

Did I tell lies? Have I unjustly or rashly accused or judged others? Did I sinby calumny (telling derogatory lies about another person), Did I engage in gossip, backbiting, or taletelling? Did I reveal a secret which was entrusted to me without due cause?

(SOURCE: "Handbook of Prayers" Scepter Publishers,NY)

## PRAYER BEFORE CONFESSION

*Oh Holy Spirit, come in Thy Mercy; enlighten my mind and strengthen my will that I may know my sins, humbly confess them, and sincerely amend my life. Mary, My Mother, Immaculate Spouse of the Holy Spirit, refuge of sinners, assist me by Thy Intercession. Holy Angels and Saints of God, pray for me! Amen.*
*Imp. Cardinal Feldmen NY, 1953*
(SOURCE: "My Prayer Book" by Fr. Lasance, Benziger Brothers Inc., NY)

# CHAPTER EIGHT

# INDULGENCES
### CCC. 1471-1479

I n my travels and discussions with Catholic parents across the country, one question I see frequently is, "What are indulgences? How can I teach my kids about them when I don't understand them myself?" I am not a theologian, but will try to give a simplified explanation of what they are and how they work. There are two times when we can endure suffering, one is after death in Purgatory, the other is during earthly life. Indulgences are granted by the Church to the faithful as a way for us to make amends for punishment due to our sins. A great example from *The Catholic Answers* tract on Indulgences is helpful here: If a teenager stays out past curfew deliberately, then arrives home very sorry and penitent, the parents may forgive the teen, but he will still be punished for his actions. When we go to confession, we are given absolution and forgiven our sins, but there still remains punishment due for them. This is the purpose of indulgences. The indulgences that the Church grants to the faithful serve to make up for the temporal punishment due to our sins after they have been forgiven in a sacramental confession.

Hundreds of years ago the Church would impose harsh punishments like wearing a hair shirt for 50 days, crawling on the knees to a nearby shrine, etc. When the Church instituted the act of indulgences, which are prayers, prayerful devotions and good works, they took the place of these harsh physical punishments. The power of granting indulgences has been given to the Church by Christ and the Church has used this divinely bestowed power even from its earliest days. Scripturally, the power for the Church to grant indulgences can be seen in the reference to the judicial authority of the Church in Matt. 16: 19, which we studied earlier in the section regarding papal authority.

There are two types of indulgences which the Church grants: *partial* and *plenary* (full). A *partial indulgence* will remove some of the temporal punishment due to our sins, while a *plenary indulgence* will literally, 'wipe our slate clean' by removing all punishment due to our sins to date. Many standard prayers have partial indulgences attached: the Hail Mary, the Holy Rosary, Consecration to the Sacred Heart, and simply saying the name of Jesus are examples. Many prayer books will state at the end of the prayer in italics or parenthesis whether the prayer has a partial or plenary indulgence. Older prayer books may say "indulgence of 500 days", "Seven Years Indulgence" etc. by using a specific time. These indulgences were revised in 1967 by Pope Paul VI and no longer have a specific time attached, but would simply be considered partial indulgences.

If we wish to gain the partial indulgence attached to a prayer or devotion, there are two conditions which must be met:

1) We must have the intention of gaining the indulgence. We can do this simply by saying a prayer every morning before we start out day:

> Oh Jesus, I wish to gain every indulgence and merit I can today and to offer them for the intentions of Your Sacred Heart.

2)  We should be in a state of grace when the actions are performed.

In order to gain the Plenary Indulgence, there are three general conditions:

1)  Make a good confession (Eight days before or afterwith firm resolve and detachment from sin)
2.) Recieve Holy Communion
3.) Add prayers on behalf of the Pope's intentions - this can be simply saying an Our Father, Hail Mary and Glory Be.

So now that we have a better grasp on why the Church grants indulgences to the faithful, it should be an inspiration to us to make a more conscious effort to gain all of the indulgences we can. The Church grants indulgences by giving them the power to remove the punishment due to our sins both in this life and the hereafter. We should all be anxious to gain partial and plenary indulgences to remove these punishments due to our sins.

The concept of indulgences is a difficult one to explain to children. One way is by using the teenage/curfew story mentioned earlier. Another helpful analogy to explain indulgences was provided for me by another mom:

When you are baptized and become a child of God, your soul becomes clean and spotless, like a white board. When you sin, it's like hammering nails into your white board. When you go to confession, it's like pulling out the nails. But even after the nails have been removed, what still remains? Holes, right? Indulgences help to fill in the holes.

This is a simplified way to explain indulgences to younger children. One time when I used it was when we were becoming lax in using the Sign of the Cross before grace. In our haste, we were often just jumping right into the prayer and neglecting the Sign of the Cross, which is an indulgenced prayerful action. I used this analogy to explain why we needed to be more careful in saying our grace, and how important and powerful the Sign of the Cross is. Do not expect your child to develop a full understanding of the power of indulgences on the level that you have acquired, just help them get the idea that indulgenced prayers are important, and include prayers you know to be indulgenced in your daily family prayers.

To find out a complete listing of indulgenced prayers and devotions, the Church has them listed in a work entitled, *The Enchiridion of Indulgences.*

This work is available on the internet to be viewed, printed or downloaded. You can locate it by doing a search on the title.

## PARTIAL INDULGENCES

One of the faithful who, being at least inwardly contrite, performs a work carrying with it a partial indulgence receives through the Church the remission of temporal punishment. A partial indulgence is granted to the faithful who:

* In the performance of their duties and in bearing the trials of life raise their minds with humble confidence to God, adding -even if only mentally - some pious invocation.

*   In a spirit of Faith and mercy give of themselves or of their goods to serve others in need.
*   In a spirit of penance voluntarily deprive themselves of what is licit and pleasing to them.
*   Devoutly use religious articles (crucifixes, rosaries, medals, scapulars) properly blessed by a priest.

## PLENARY INDULGENCES

One may gain a plenary indulgence under the normal prerequisites by:

*   Visiting the Blessed Sacrament for half an hour
*   Visiting any parish Church

a)  On the Day of the titular feast of the church
b)  On August 2, the day of the "Portiuncula indulgence," or on another suitable day to be fixed by the local ordinary
c)  On November 2 (applicable to the dead only)

On these visits one should recite the Our Father, and the Creed and fulfill the ealier mentioned requirements (confession, communion, prayer for Pope's intentions, and have a sincere desire to improve.)

*   Reading the Bible for at least half and hour.
*   Making the Stations of the Cross.
*   Praying the Rosary in a church or with one's family.
*   Receiving the Apostolic Blessing at the hour of death.

("Handbook of Prayers" - Scepter Pub, Inc. 20 Nassau St., Princeton, NJ)

CHAPTER NINE

# THE ALL MALE PRIESTHOOD
## CCC. 1577

A natural question your child may ask is wh women cannot be priests. This has been a very strongly held practice since Jesus founded His Church. Let's look at some Scriptural references to this belief:

> As in all the churches of the holy ones, women should keep silent in the churches, for they are not allowed to speak, but should be subordinate, even as the law says.
>
> —1 Cor. 14: 34-35

This passage does not mean that women should not attend church and pray. It alludes to the fact that women should not be in the position to publicly lead the prayers and preach, which are the duties of a priest. In 1 Cor. 11: 1-16, it clearly states that woman can publicly pray and even prophesy. These passages should not be misunderstood to mean that women should have no voice or function within the Church.

> A woman must receive instruction silently and under complete control. I do not permit a woman to teach or have authority over a man.
>
> —1 Tim. 2: 11-14

In saying "teach" here, St. Paul is not referring to the literal act of teaching or instruction in education. He is referring to one of the primary priestly duties: preaching.

These Scriptural references are clear, but perhaps an even better argument against women priests is to simply look at what Jesus Himself did while on earth. Jesus, the true High Priest, chose twelve men to be his apostles, and ultimately the first priests and bishops of the Catholic Church.

He had a very holy company of women who travelled with Him during His public ministry, including St. Mary Magdalene, St. Veronica, and of course, the holiest woman of all, The Blessed Mother. One could argue that these women were, at times, even more courageous and devoted to Our Lord than most of His apostles by the fact that 11 of the 12 apostles deserted Jesus during His crucifixion, but the Holy Women remained with Him beneath the cross. However, Jesus did not choose any of these wonderfully holy women to be leaders of His Church.

Today, Feminists within the Church charge that because of the "cultural norms" of his day, Jesus couldn't choose women because it just wouldn't have been acceptable. This is an especially weak excuse for not following Our Lord's example. Jesus was God incarnate - He could see down through all time the effect that each of His actions would ultimately have upon His Church. Surely He knew that the question of women priests would arise in the future. If He intended for women to eventually become priests, He would have most certainly set the example by choosing women from among His holy company to be the first women priests. Jesus was not above preaching against the cultural norms of the day anyway; just look at how scandalized the crowds were when He explained that we would have to eat His Body and drink His Blood in order to have eternal life. Cultural norms of the day certainly did not support such doctrine, but Jesus preached it vocally nonetheless.

There are those within the Church who argue that a woman cannot 'be complete' until she is permitted to become a priest. This is a bit of an insult to those many women through history who have lived saintly lives as mothers, nuns and celibate single women in great service of His Church. A modern day example is Mother Angelica. This nun has single-handedly instituted the largest Catholic television network in the world! The effect of her outreach efforts for evangelization within our Church are felt in all four corners of the earth. Is Mother Angelica incomplete because she cannot become a priest? Could she do *more* as a priest? I certainly doubt it!

Look at all of the incredible women saints in the glorious history of our Church who have had major impacts through their writings and teachings, including St. Catherine of Sienna and St. Teresa of Avila, who were Doctors of the Church. Certainly to say that they could not fully serve the Church because they could not become priests is faulty thinking.

Furthermore, Pope John Paul II recently *infallibly* defined in *Ordinatio Sacerdotalis* that only men can be ordained priests. This is now a doctrine of our faith which cannot be altered in any way by any future popes. This is the definitive 'last word' on the subject and should be enough to put the issue of women priests to rest once and for all. In this apostolic letter the Pope states very eloquently about the role of women within our Church:

> By defending the dignity of women and their vocation, the Church has shown honor and

> gratitude for those women who—faithful to
> the Gospel—have shared in every age in the
> apostolic mission of the whole People of God.
> They are the holy martyrs, virgins, and the
> mothers of families, who bravely bore witness
> to their faith and passed on the Church's faith
> and tradition by bringing up their children in
> the spirit of the Gospel.
> (Sec. 11 of Ordinatio Sacerdotalis).

When children ask why women cannot become priests, the explanation of what Jesus did is the simplest way to clarify this point. I also recommend we instill in our children a healthy and elevated notion of one of the major vocations of a Catholic woman: to become a mother. Motherhood is demeaned so highly in our society today. Women are made to feel that we cannot be complete until we have careers outside of the home. Infuse in your children that a woman has many options in her life in which to serve Our Lord and His Church. One is to be a wife and mother. We cannot deny one simple truth: Jesus himself chose to be born into this world of a woman.

This act alone is a testament to the prominent vocation of motherhood. St. Timothy speaks so highly of this wonderful vocation:

> I will therefore that the younger should marry,
> bear children, be mistresses of families, give
> no occasion to the adversary to speak evil.
> —1 Tim. 5: 14

Other references to motherhood and its blessings abound in Scripture. Here are a couple more that I have found to be very useful:

Yet she be saved through childbearing; if she
continue in faith, and love, and sanctification,
with sobriety.

—1 Tim 2: 13-15

Behold, the inheritance of the Lord are
children: the reward, the fruit of the just.

—Ps. 126: 3

I try to instill in my girls that being a full-time wife
and mother is a wonderful vocation for them, and that I hope
they will have the joys of such a calling some day. Another
vocation that women may wish to pursue is that of becoming
a nun. In this instance, a woman devotes her life to service
of Our Lord and His Church by forsaking a husband and
family, becoming a bride to Christ Himself. We have many
wonderful, dedicated nuns who serve our parish and school,
and I make sure my children understand what a sacrifice
these women make to serve our Church by choosing such a
vocation. A third option for a woman is to live a dedicated,
chaste life of a single person. All of these preferences for a
lifestyle vocation are wonderful and pleasing to God. We
must lead our children to see this belief and help them each
discover their own vocation in life.

## DISCUSSING THE SUBJECT OF VOCATION WITH YOUR CHILDREN

As parents, we must constantly be aware of our words
and actions when we discuss the vocation of the priesthood or
religious life. It is said that St. John Vianney once commented
that if he was walking along and came across an angel and
a priest, he would bow down in reverence to the priest, for
he is the one with the ability to transform the simple bread
and wine into the Body, Blood, Soul and Divinity of Jesus

Christ. Not even an angel in heaven has this ability! What a powerful thought that is to impress on our children. Instill in them a reverence and respect for the priesthood, for these men arecalled by God to a life of sacrifice and giving in order for us to be blessed with the Sacraments. Without the priests, we would not have the Holy Mass, the forgiveness of sins through Confession, the important Sacrament of the Sick for times of serious illness, nor the welcoming into God's Family of our babies during Baptism. We would be deprived of so many critical spiritual avenues for grace in our lives.

When discussing the vocation of the priesthood (or religious life), instill in the children the understanding that although they may 'give up' the life choice of a spouse and children, God will reward them beyond their imaginings for such a sacrifice in service of His Kingdom. The parish that they are called to serve (if they are a diocesan priest or religious) becomes their 'family.' A life seeking a religious vocation also may involve missionary work and traveling the world to bring the truth of the Faith to those who have not yet heard the Good News.

When my husband's old roommate from college, who is now a priest, stopped by recently to visit, I mentioned to him that we were trying to 'plant the seed' with our son to consider a religious vocation. Fr. Pat talked with him and told him what a great life he was enjoying as a priest. I believe it made a profound impact on our son.

He later said that he was thinking about it - something he had never admitted before. Although he is only 10, it is not too soon to instill in him the awareness of the religious life as a possible vocation. Speak positively to your children about religious vocations and do not neglect to pray daily that they will be lead to the vocation in life which will bring God the greatest honor and glory.

# CHAPTER TEN

# PRIESTLY CELIBACY
### CCC. 1577

There may come a time when one of your children will ask you why it is that Catholic priests are not married and do not have children. Since it's likely that your child will be referring to your parish priest, I will assume that parents referring to this book here in America are largely Roman Catholic, part of the Latin Rite Church. For your own information, it is helpful for us to know, although, that the priestly celibacy rule does not apply to *all* Catholic priests. For exceptions to this rule and a more detailed explanation of Eastern Rite Catholic chuches and their tenets regarding married clergy, please see the Appendix section. In Roman Catholic churches, the celibacy rule had become mandatory by the early Middle Ages. This is what's known as a 'disciplinary rule,' not a doctrine.

One reason it is the preferred state for Latin Rite Catholic priests is because of the number of scriptural references which refer to the efficacy of priestly celibacy. First and foremost, Jesus, the High Priest, chose a life of celibacy. Even though Jesus Himself elevated marriage to a sacrament, He clearly indicates the necessity of a priest leading a life of celibacy in total devotion to serving the flock of His Church. Here are some of the Scriptural references to the celibacy rule: (*Jesus speaking on remaining celibate*).

> ...Not all can accept this word, but only
> those to whom that is granted. ...some have
> renounced marriage for the sake of the
> kingdom of heaven. Whoever can accept this
> ought to accept it.'
>
> —Matt. 19: 11-12

When Jesus speaks of men who will be called to renounce marriage for the sake of the kingdom, he is clearly referring to those who will be called to serve in the highest way as priests. Later in the same passage, Jesus speaks of the importance of 'leaving everything' to follow Him.

This also seems to clearly support the discipline of giving up a family and marriage in order to serve as a priest. Furthermore, St. Paul also advocated a life of celibacy in service of the kingdom:

> Now to the unmarried and to widows I say:
> it is a good thing for them to remain as they
> do, as I do....
>
> —1 Cor. 7: 8-9

> I want you to be free from anxieties. The
> unmarried man is anxious about the affairs
> of the Lord, how to please the Lord; but the
> married man is anxious about worldly affairs,
> how to please his wife, and his interests are
> divided...
>
> —1 Cor. 7: 32-35

Here St. Paul reiterates what a strain it would be fore a married man with a family to fully serve the Church.

When my daughter asked why Fr. George wasn't

married and did not have children, I explained something like this:

> You know that Fr. George is very busy. He celebrates Masses everyday and many Masses on the weekends. During that time he also hears confessions, counsels various people, visits the sick and dying, and has many other duties. If daddy was a priest and was that busy, how would he ever be able to find time for us? He would never be able to go to see your soccer games on the weekends, or take vacations with us, or do many things that daddies need to do with their families. A priest's life is totally devoted to serving the people in his parish - they become his children' and family. If he had a wife and other children waiting at home, they would suffer and not have time with him. Or if he had a wife and children and paid too much attention to them, then the parish would suffer and not have a priest there to do all the duties God has called them to do.

This simplified explanation really brought home to my daughter how much a priest does for his parish, as well as how much of a sacrifice they make in serving a life of celibacy in total devotion to the service of the Church.

# A PRAYER FOR VOCATIONS

*Lord Jesus Christ, Shepherd of Souls, who called the apostles to be fishers of men, raise up new apostles in your holy Church. Teach them that to serve you is to reign: to possess you is to possess all things. Kindle in the hearts of our young people the fire of zeal for souls. Make them eager to spread your Kingdom upon earth. Grant them courage to follow you, who are the Way, the Truth, and the Life; who live and reign forever and ever. Amen.*

(SOURCE: "Handbook of Prayers" - Scepter Pub, Inc.)

# CHAPTER ELEVEN

# SACRAMENTALS AND RELICS
CCC. 1667 - 1673

As Catholic people, one of the greatest treasures we have are sacramentals and relics. Here are some examples of common and well known sacramentals: the Sign of the Cross, the Stations of the Cross, holy water, blessed candles and ashes, Crucifixes and Crosses, the Rosary, the scapular, and holy medals of the saints. Relics are actual pieces of a saint's body (*First Class relics*), or actual items which the saint was known to possess or use on earth such as clothing, holy books, etc. (*Second Class relics*). Another type of relic is called *Third Class*, and refers to any object (i.e. a small piece of cloth) which has been touched directly to a First or Second Class relic. Many sacramentals, like some saints' medals, contain relics. We honor relics because Scripture tells us of their efficacy:

> So Elisha died, and they buried him. Now bands of Moabites used to invade the land in the spring of the year. And as a man was being buried, lo, a marauding band was seen and the man was cast into the grave of Elisha; and as soon as the man touched the bones of Elisha, he revived, and stood on his feet.
> —2 Kings: 13:20-21

We see other references to relics and their power in the New Testament:

> And God did extraordinary miracles by the hands of Paul, so that handkerchiefs or aprons were carried away from his body to the sick, and diseases left them and the evil spirits came out of them.
>
> —Acts 19: 11-12

The Early Church employed the belief in relics by the fact that they kept the burial cloth of Christ, portions of the True Cross which Jesus was crucified upon, and have jealously guarded and saved bones and belongings of various saints down through the ages.

A *sacramental* is anything which has been set apart or blessed by the Church to increase devotion and bring our minds and hearts to good thoughts. We believe that the prayers that the Church says over sacramentals move God to give graces and bestow gifts of protection and health upon the faithful. When I encourage mothers and fathers to have sacramentals around their homes, especially blessed Rosaries, scapulars, and holy medals, it's important to clarify how such objects should be used. When you purchase new Rosaries or holy medals for your children to wear, make sure to have them blessed first by a Bishop, priest or deacon. It is this blessing on behalf of the Church that calls God's blessings upon the object. There are remarkable effects which are attributed to sacramentals, one of which is the ability to drive away evil spirits. The Church combats the powers of the occult by blessed sacramentals, most notably holy water, St. Benedict's medals, and blessed salt. Another power of sacramentals is that they may be employed for use by the faithful to obtain temporal favors, such as the practice of burying a statue of St.

Joseph in the yard of a home when the owners wish to find a suitable buyer.

Sacramentals should not be used in a manner that is superstitious. One way that would be considered a sinful use of a sacramental is if one used it and believed he would be saved by its use, despite a sinful life. For example, a young man wears a brown scapular because his grandmother promised that if he did, he would go to heaven after death. The young man wears it faithfully, but otherwise lives a sinful life and neglects the sacraments of faith. This is using a sacramental in a way that is superstitious and sinful. Another example would be if an individual buried a statue of St. Joseph in his front yard in hopes of selling his home, but did it superstitiously and without any type of prayer or devotion to accompany such an act.

The use of sacramentals by the faithful must be accompanied by an effort to live a good and virtuous life in imitation of the Gospel. The faithful use of sacramentals within the home is one which Catholics must try to restore.

It is simple enough by starting with the basics: having holy water fonts available, scapulars for all family members after they have made First Communion, patron saints or favorite saints' holy medals for children to wear, and a family altar with blessed candles and images. When purchasing sacramentals, it's important to note that the Church prohibits the sale of items which have been blessed. That is why many missions will offer medals and Rosaries which have been blessed *for donation only*. Most missions will have it clearly marked somewhere on the package that the item(s) have been blessed. If it does not specifically say that it has been blessed, or has been purchased at a local Catholic bookstore, you are responsible to have your local priest bless it before its use by your family.

I particularly urge all parents to wear and have their families wear the brown scapular of Our Lady of Mt. Carmel. It is necessary to be officially enrolled in the Scapular Confraternity, after which you no longer need to have subsequent scapulars which you will wear in the future blessed. Twenty years ago, it was standard for most priests to automatically enroll children in the brown scapular after they made their First Holy Communion. Unfortunately, this is yet another wonderful tradition that many priests no longer practice, and you may need to actively seek out a priest in order to have him read the words of enrollment into the brown scapular. The formula for enrollment into the brown scapular is available in the appendix section.

Some comments I encounter when I talk to people about the importance of wearing the brown scapular are, "It's too bothersome to wear," "It gets tangled in my jewelry," etc. When our Lady appeared as Our Lady of Mt. Carmel in her apparition at Fatima, she did not speak words. She was pictured holding out a brown scapular - an obvious message that she prefers her children to wear one. She never said it would always be convenient - she just requests that we do it. The same goes for those who say that they 'don't get anything out of it' when they try to say the daily Rosary. Once again, we should just remember that Our Lady asks us to do it.

If your children ever complain about saying a family Rosary because they find it boring, use this analogy:

> If your mother asked you to go out into her garden and pick 50 roses for her, would you do it? Or would you say, "No, mom, I'm sorry, I just don't get anything out of picking roses. I might hurt my fingers on a thorn. I'd rather not." When Our Lady asks us to do things

like saying the Rosary and wearing a scapular, it's because it's best for us. These things help us to become special members in Our Lady's prayerful army. Even though we don't always feel something special from saying a Rosary, she still asks us to do it as a favor for her everyday. We should do it just because she asks us to, and she will reward us.

Another extraordinary reason to wear the brown Scapular is the *Sabbatine Privilege*. This Privilege is a promise from the Blessed Mother that She will release from Purgatory on the first Saturday (hence the name "Sabbatine") after death all those who wear the brown Scapular, observe chastity according to their state in life, and say the Little Office of the Blessed Virgin or the Rosary daily. What an exceptional promise which clearly shows how Our Lady rewards those faithful who wear Her garment of grace, the brown Scapular.

Finally, teach your children to respect objects and sacramentals that have been blessed. When a blessed Rosary has been dropped, have them pick it up and reverently kiss the crucifix. Do the same if their saint's medals are dropped. When they go swimming or bathe, have them remove their brown scapular to avoid getting it wet. When a scapular has been worn to the point of being smelly and dirty, wash it out or don a new one. You can take old scapulars that are too worn or dirty to wear and bury them in the four corners of your property for special protection. You can also place them under your mattresses. Do not throw away sacramentals that have been blessed if you no longer wish to use them. Store them, or place them in areas around your home for added protection because they are blessed. To learn more about the incredible variety of sacramentals and their powers and graces, I highly recommend the booklet, *Our Lady Teaches About Sacramentals and Blessed Objects.*

# CHAPTER TWELVE

# THE POPE AND PAPAL INFALLIBILITY
## CCC. 85, 2032 - 2034

L et's start this chapter with a primary belief of our Faith: we have a Pope, who was commissioned by Jesus Christ himself, to lead our Church. We need to foster in our children a great respect for this visible head of the Catholic Church on earth. This section will deal with three issues related to the Pope: the need for a single leader, Jesus' actual selection of the first Pope, Peter, and the issue of infallibility. Begin by explaining to children the whole idea of papal succession in its simplest terms: Jesus chose one of his twelve apostles, St. Peter, to be the first Pope of our Church. We can see this in Scripture:

> And so I say to you, you are Peter, and upon this rock I will build my church, and the gates of the netherworld shall not prevail against it. I will give you the keys to the kingdom of heaven. Whatever you bind on earth shall be bound in heaven, and whatever you loose on earth shall be loosed in heaven.
>
> —Matt. 16: 18-20

This passage shows a few important things: Jesus makes a dramatic statement here by changing Simon's name to Peter, which means 'rock.' Jesus also promises that the Church Peter will head will be one which even the gates of hell (netherworld) shall never defeat. Jesus uses the words referring to giving Peter the keys to the kingdom of heaven. This is a reference to an Old Testament reference in which the key to the house of David' is mentioned, (Is. 22, 15-25). This reference to a key is a symbol of authority, a prefiguring to the fact that Peter as pope will have authority over this Church. And finally, Jesus makes a special promise directly to Peter.

He tells Peter that as leader of this Church, whatever Peter binds on earth will also be bound in heaven, and whatever he declares loosed on earth shall be loosed in heaven. This is a promise from Jesus that he will protect his Church from error by giving the Pope the power to make infallible proclamations on behalf of the Church regarding issues of faith and morals.

*Infallibility* is the inability of the Church to teach error in the area of faith and morals. It is not, as many Protestants misunderstand, a declaration that the Pope cannot sin. The Pope is a human being and certainly capable of sin. But as a defense for this Church, Jesus promised that when the Pope speaks on behalf of the Church on issues of faith or morals, he will speak free from error. This also extends to statements made by the *bishops when they are in union with the pope* on these same issues. Thus, the Catholic Church is preserved from error, and the gates of hell will not prevail against it. The Scripture quotes supporting infallibility are numerous. In one verse, Jesus promises the Holy Spirit to be the guide of his Church:

> But when he comes, the Spirit of truth, he will guide you to all truth.
> —John 16:13

This promise by Jesus that his Spirit will always lead the Church to be free from error gives a guarantee that the one, true Church will not fall away from his authentic teachings:

> But if I should be delayed, you should know
> how to behave in the household of God, which
> is the church of the living God, the pillar and
> foundation of truth.
> —1 Tim. 3:15

It doesn't take long to figure out why we need one definitive leader for the Church that Jesus founded. Just look around at the many hundreds of different Protestant churches: One supports abortion, another is against it. One says homosexuality is acceptable, while another says it is a lifestyle that God never intended. They each believe they are correct and are interpreting scripture to suit their beliefs. There is no definitive voice for any of them; they are, in effect, each 'doing their own thing'. Who's right? In the Catholic Church, we are safeguarded from such varied and conflicting interpretations by the fact that we have our Pope and teaching Magisterium to teach us clearly what the faithful are to believe. This does not mean that individual priests and church leaders will not attempt to break away from official church teachings and insist on false interpretations of various issues. These individuals within the church who are 'doing their own thing' are not in communion with the Pope or teaching Magisterium. Even though some of these groups may insist that they are "Catholic," if their stance on issues are not in agreement with the teachings of the Pope and the constant teachings of the Church, they are rejecting Jesus and His true Church. Jesus said, when speaking to Peter and the apostles as the first leaders of His Church:

> Whoever listens to you listens to me. Whoever
> rejects you rejects me. And whoever rejects me
> rejects the one who sent me.
> —Luke 10: 16

Scripture further illustrates that Jesus intended Peter to be the first of many Popes to lead the Church by another passage:

> He (Jesus) said to him (Peter), Feed my lambs.'
> He then said to him a second time, Simon, son of John, do you love me?' He said to him, Tend my sheep.' He said to him a third time, Simon, son of John, do you love me?' Peter was distressed that he had said to him a third time, Do you love me?' and he said, Lord, you know everything; you know I love you.' Jesus said to him, Feed my sheep.
> —John 21: 15-18

These three references to Peter feeding the sheep and tending the flock are cited by the First Vatican Council as proof that Jesus was giving Peter jurisdiction of supreme shepherd and ruler over the whole flock (the Church). Jesus asked Peter three times if Peter loved Him because Peter had denied Jesus three times prior to the crucifixion. There has been an unbroken line of Popes from Peter to our present Pope John Paul II. As an activity with older children, see if you can locate a listing showing all the Popes from Peter to our present Pope.

Also, make it a point to teach your children about the need for us to pray for our Pope frequently and for his intentions. Because our Pope carries the weight of the world on his shoulders, he is in constant need of the prayers of the faithful to support him. What a gift our Lord gave to His Church by giving us these doctrines of Papal Authority and Papal Infallibility. By such doctrines we can be assured that our Church cannot teach heresy and error. We are blessed with the truth which is only found in its most complete way in the one, holy, Catholic and Apostolic Church.

CHAPTER THIRTEEN

# THE PRACTICE OF CHASTITY
CCC. 2351- 2355

Chastity and abstinence from a sexual relationship before marriage will not likely be a topic of discussion with your children until they become teenagers. It is hoped that we will constantly live our own lives as Catholic parents in a way that will daily attest to the beauty and sanctity of whatever our state in life may be: married, divorced, or widowed. However, we live in a society that believes it's best to teach our children that the only kind of sex is "safe sex" and that teens "are going to do it anyway, so let's teach them how to do it so they don't get AIDS or pregnant." What an insult our current sex ed programs are to our teens - to tell them that they are a bunch of animals who cannot control themselves, so they'd better at least 'use protection' since they are going to have sex. Even if your kids are not in public school or sex ed programs, they will still be bombarded with sexual messages and daily assaults against their purity. We must arm them with the truths from a very young age regarding the need to remain chaste and abstain from having a sexual relationship until they are blessed to enter into a sacramental Catholic marriage.

How or when you tell your younger child about sex is up to you and the children's age and maturity levels. We found the best way to address natural curiosities was when I became pregnant. It's a natural time to address issues related to fetal growth and development. One of the biggest mistakes parents today are making is telling their little ones TOO much about sex - more than they actually need or care to know. When your youngster asks where babies come from, that doesn't necessarily mean we must go into a complete physiological/biological explanation of the 'birds and the bees.' Often, a simple explanation is the best and guards the purity of your child:

> When a husband and wife love each other very much, sometimes they share a special love together. When they have this special love, sometimes God will give them a baby because of it. This special love is a gift from God, and it is only meant for a husband and wife who are married.

There may certainly arise occasions when your child will become aware of a woman who is having a baby, but is not married. Again, for young children, a simple explanation will suffice:

> Well, you know how we talked about the special kind of love that a husband and wife have together when they are married? Sometimes, when the mommy and daddy have this special love, they are given the gift of a baby. The special love is a gift from God that is meant for married people. Sometimes, though, a young man and woman decide to have this special love before they are married. This is wrong and greatly hurts God. They are abusing the gift of special love that God made especially for married people. That's what happened to so-and-so. They shared

the special kind of love before marriage and now they have a baby. It's not the baby's fault and that baby is still a very precious gift from God.

As your kids grow, they may come to question why it is necessary to remain chaste before marriage. Here are some Biblical exhortations to the practice of chastity:

> Take heed to keep thyself, my son, from all fornication (*Fornication refers to sex outside of marriage*), and beside thy wife, never endure to know a crime.
> —Tob. 4:13

> I beseech you, therefore, brethren, by the mercy of God, that you present your bodies a living sacrifice, holy, pleasing unto God, your reasonable service.
> —Rom. 12:1

> For this is the will of God, your sanctification; that you should abstain from fornication; That every one of you should know how to possess his vessel in sanctification and honor.
> —1 Thess. 4: 3-5

> Not in the passion of lust, like the Gentiles that know not God, for God hath not called us unto uncleanness, but unto sanctification. Therefore he that despiseth these things, despiseth not man, but God, who also hath given his holy Spirit in us.
> —1 Thess. 4: 7, 8

Keep thyself chaste.

—1 Tim 5: 22

Dearly beloved, I beseech you as strangers and pilgrims, to refrain yourselves from carnal desires which war against the soul.

—1 Peter 2: 11

There are a number of strong references in Scripture to the danger of living in a state of fornication. Unfortunately, when these Scripture verses are read, we often fail to explain to our kids what fornication means!

Do not err: neither fornicators, nor idolaters, nor adulterers...shall possess the kingdom of God.

—1 Cor 6: 9,10

Now the works of the flesh are manifest, which are fornication, uncleanness, immodesty, ...of which I tell you as I have foretold to you, that they who do such things shall not obtain the kingdom of God.

—Gal 5: 19, 21

For know you this and understand, that no fornicator, or unclean, or covetous person hath inheritance in the kingdom of Christ and of God.

—Eph. 5: 5

Helping our children understand the sanctity of the sexual union is critical to helping them develop a mindset to stay chaste until marriage. We must help them to see from the earliest age that sex is a very special gift from God that is reserved to those who are called to live within the sacrament of marriage. The fruit of sex is often children, one reason that sex is reserved for a married couple. The 'safe sex' nonsense that is being pushed upon our children must be replaced by a simple and healthy understanding: the reason you should stay chaste until marriage isn't just to avoid getting a sexually transmitted disease, AIDS, or having a baby, it MUST be because sex is a gift reserved for marriage.

To partake of sex before marriage is like opening up a gift before its time. God gives this special gift to a husband and wife. If you do not have the maturity level combined with the blessings and graces of a marriage, sex is just an act - a selfish one that destroys the beautiful union it was meant to be. It is also a grave sin - a mortal sin that can literally result in the loss of heaven for all eternity.

CHAPTER FOURTEEN

# HOMOSEXUALITY
CCC. 2357

I n our current society, there is a great focus in the media, television and movies on what are euphemistically termed, "alternate lifestyles." What such double speech terms are actually referring to is the homosexual lifestyle, or variations thereof. Chances are that no matter how you attempt to shield your children, they will come to you asking, "Mommy, what does 'gay' mean?" It's almost impossible to avoid. Therefore, it's important for us to fully realize why Scripture expressly condemns this lifestyle, especially when we are bombarded with messages from society telling us to be tolerant' and accepting regarding them. The Scripture passages which firmly speak against a homosexual lifestyle are most clear:

> You shall not lie with a male as with a woman; such a thing is an abomination.
> —Lev. 18:22-23

> Therefore, God handed them over to degrading passions. Their females exchanged natural relations for unnatural, and the males likewise gave up natural relations with females and burned with lust for one another. Males did shameful things with males and thus

> received in their own persons the due penalty
> for their perversions.
>
> —Rom. 1:26-27

> Do you not know that the unjust will not
> inherit the kingdom of God? Do not be
> deceived; neither fornicators nor idolaters nor
> adulterers nor boy prostitutes nor sodomites ...
> will inherit the kingdom of God.
>
> —1 Cor. 6:9

In the last verse, the term "sodomites" is translated to refer to adult males who indulged in homosexual practices. There are other very explicit references to homosexuality in Scripture. Also, as negative proof that such a lifestyle was not pleasing to God, nowhere in Scripture can even one reference be found to support such a lifestyle or indicate that it was acceptable to God. References for marriage as the natural state for a man and woman abound throughout Scripture, and Jesus elevated it to a sacrament. The gay lifestyle, no matter how "loving" or "caring" it may be, cannot be considered a substitute for the purposes of a sacramental marriage between a man and a woman. A homosexual relationship cannot ever result in one of the main purposes of the sexual union as intended by God: the procreation of children.

The Catholic Church does not condemn a person for professing to be a homosexual. The stand of the Church is "hate the sin, love the sinner." The Church does not say it is sinful to *be* homosexual, only when one engages in homosexual behavior is it considered to be gravely sinful. Just as the Church expects a heterosexual who is not married to remain chaste and not participate in fornication, so also does the Church require a homosexual to live a life of chastity and to offer up the burden in unity with the Cross of Christ.

If your child approaches and asks what gay means, keep it simple in a Biblical way:

> Gay means when a man loves a man or a woman loves a woman in the same way that mommy and daddy love each other. God gave a husband and wife a special kind of love to share when they are married. Sometimes when the husband and wife love each in the special way, God gives them a baby. Two men or two women can't ever have a baby. It takes a mommy and a daddy. When two men or two women try to love each other in the special way God meant for a husband and wife, it is a sin. This is what it means to be "gay" or "homosexual." It is a lifestyle that is not pleasing to God. God did not make two Adam's or two Eve's in the garden of Eden. He made a man and woman. We do not hate people who are gay, we just pray for them. God in His Mercy will be their judge. We pray that their hearts and minds will be opened to see that a gay lifestyle is a great sin against God and His creation.

Such an explanation can be given more or less detail with your own children, depending on their age, the depth of their questions, and how much you wish for them to know about the act of procreation in general.

# CHAPTER FIFTEEN

# BIRTH CONTROL AND STERILIZATION
## CCC. 2364-2372

One of the most misunderstood teachings of the Catholic Church, even among Catholics, is the teaching against artificial contraception and sterilization. It's interesting to note that prior to the 1930's *all major Christian religions* condemned these practices, not just the Catholic Church. It was the Anglican Church that first changed its stance to meet the popular demand of the day, after which all Protestant denominations quickly followed suit. Today, the Catholic Church stands alone in condemning these practices. The reason is quite simple: when something is inherently right, you don't change it.

Before we explore the authentic Church teaching regarding this topic, let's refer to Scripture, where we find an explicit reference to *coitus interruptus* and its consequences:

> Onan, however, knew that the descendants would not be counted as his; so whenever he had relations with his brother's widow, he wasted his seed on the ground to avoid contributing offspring for his brother. What he did greatly offended the Lord, and the Lord took his life, too.
>
> —Gen. 38: 9-10

Less explicit references are made against sterilization in the book of Deuteronomy. Furthermore, the earliest Church Fathers refer to the sinful nature of the practices of sterility, abortion and birth control, including Barnabas, Clement of Alexandria and Hippolytus.

It's imperative that we, as Catholic parents, understand the Church's infallible teachings regarding these 'hot-button' issues of artificial contraception and sterilization.

Since recent studies show that over 75% of Catholic couples do not follow the Church's instructions regarding this issue, we are certainly raising another generation of Catholics who will likely also disregard these truths. The Church has always upheld the belief that children are a blessing. Nowhere in Scripture, in fact, can you find references to the contrary. The Church came out in the 1960's with its infallible and clear declaration on the purposes of the marital act in Pope Paul VI's Encyclical entitled, *Humane Vitae*. This IS the pronouncement which spells out all the evils of contraception and sterilization.

Humane Vitae explains that there are two main purposes for the sexual union within a marriage: *unitive* and *procreative*. Both are equally important and both purposes must be present each time a married couple joins in the marital act. The *unitive* aspect is to manifest their affection and to safeguard their mutual fidelity, giving proof to a truly honest love. The *procreative* purpose requires the couple to always remain open to the will of God and the possibility that the union may result in a new life. Any type of artificial contraception or sterilization of either the husband or wife, in order to avoid pregnancy automatically eliminates this procreative purpose. Once stripped of the aspect of procreation, physical pleasure is left. The couple has frustrated the intent for which God created the maritial union. To do so is a grave sin.

When a couple gets married in the Catholic Church, they make a vow to remain open to life and to the possible gift of children. They invite God into the equation of their lifelong commitment to each other. It is no longer just a husband and wife, but becomes a triangular relationship - God, husband and wife. Any use of contraceptive devices or procedures opposes this vow, and automatically removes God from the equation. Artificial birth control and sterilization take away all possible creative power from God.

The Church does give Catholic couples options for spacing and limiting the size of their families in cases of necessity. The Church allows couples to use knowledge garnished from learning about their own fertility in a natural way. This type of instruction approved by the Church for Catholic couples is called Natural Family Planning (NFP).

There are several methods of NFP which vary in philosophy and practice, but all of which are Church approved, including the Creighton Model of NFP and the Couple to Couple League's Sympto-Thermal Method. NFP is not "the Rhythm Method". Unfortunately, many people today still mistakenly believe that the "Rhythm Method" and NFP are synonymous. They are not. The so called "Rhythm Method" attempted to guess a woman's fertile time by simply counting out days on a calendar. Modern methods of NFP are far more sophisticated and accurate.

During NFP instruction, a couple learns about their natural combined fertility, and they can use that knowledge to either avoid *or* achieve a pregnancy. Thus, NFP is *not* a method of artificial birth control. In fact, as a method of avoiding a pregnancy, NFP is a highly effective method and has shown to be more effective than many types of artificial birth control currently on the market.

Some will ask why it is approved for a couple to use NFP to avoid a pregnancy, while artificial methods and sterilization are not acceptable. The difference is that when a couple uses NFP to avoid a pregnancy, they do not resort to the use of anything artificial: drugs, sterilization, surgery, or devices. NFP simply provides the knowledge that a couple needs to most effectively identify their combined time of fertility each cycle. They can then choose to avoid having intercourse during this fertile time, if it is their desire to avoid a pregnancy or space pregnancies for good reasons. Thus, they postpone the act of intercourse until a different time in the cycle, when both purposes of the union can again be present: the unitive and the procreative. The couple who uses birth control or sterilization does not permit the procreative purpose to be present during their union.

It's interesting to note that Pope Paul VI wrote *Humane Vitae* to reinforce Church teaching on this subject, but he was also quite prophetic. He wrote that if widespread use of contraception came into practice, the result would be an increase in sexual promiscuity, marital infidelity and divorce, abortion, and even euthanasia. All of these things have certainly come to pass since contraception became the law of the land.

It's also interesting that many Protestants are coming around today to see the truth in these teachings of the Catholic Church. Currently, many evangelical Protestants are returning to the historically correct position against contraception which the Church has always upheld.

If your older child or teen begins asking questions about this topic, it's time to reinforce both the sanctity of the marital union, as well as the Church's teachings regarding celibacy until marriage. Girls who have begun experiencing monthly periods can even begin an introduction to the basics of NFP charting, in which a woman charts her daily signs of fertility. By this I mean a simple and basic explanation of what the charting is all about: the different phases of a woman's cycle and how they relate to a couple's combined fertility. Again, the depth of the explanation will vary depending on general knowledge and maturity level of your children.

The most important thing I hope moms reading this section will obtain is the need to inform yourself about this critical issue. There are still so many parents today who wish to live in the light of the truth of the teachings of our faith, but who falter when it comes to this particular issue because they do not fully understand it. Educate yourself and read the beautifully written encyclical, *Humane Vitae*. It is not a difficult document to read, and so fully explores this issue with such lucid explanations that it will likely dispel any doubts that this is the truth by which Catholic parents must live. For myself, I found that every time I thought the Catholic Church had it wrong, it was because I had not fully explored and learned the Church's true position and teachings. When I explored through reading and self education, I always came to the same conclusion: *the Catholic Church is always right!*

# CHAPTER SIXTEEN

# PRAYING TO THE
# SAINTS AND ANGELS
## CCC. 2683-2684

O ne of the main practices which Protestants often greatly
misunderstand is the custom of praying to the saints
and angels for intercession. We believe that the angels and
saints in heaven not only pray with us, but also *for* us. The
saints in heaven have the ability to offer up to God the prayers
of the faithful on earth. This may be seen by a passage from
St. John the Evangelist in the Book of Revelations:

> ....the twenty-four elders (the leaders of the
> people of God in heaven) fell down before the
> Lamb, each holding a harp, and with golden
> bowls full of incense, which are the prayers of
> the saints.
>
> —Rev. 5:8

The angels also are mentioned as doing essentially the
same thing:

> An angel came and stood at the altar in heaven
> with a golden censer; and he was given much
> incense to mingle with the prayers of all the
> saints upon the golden altar before the throne;
> and the smoke of the incense rose with the

prayers of the saints from the hand of the
angel before God.

—Rev. 8: 3-4

The Protestants who have a problem with Catholics
giving honor to and praying for intercession from the angels
and saints usually mention one passage to support their
position: 1 Tim. 2:5 in which Jesus is mentioned as the only
Mediator between man and God.

This verse is very true, Jesus is the sole Mediator, but
this does not mean that we are restricted from asking our
fellow Christians to pray both for us and with us. This would
also include our fellow Christians in heaven and in Purgatory,
who are all a part of the body of Christ: the Church.

If you are ever asked by a Protestant why we pray to
the saints, ask them this:

> If your mother was very ill, would you come
> to me and ask me to join you in prayer for her?
> If you would come to me, a mere person, a
> sinning human being, and ask me to intercede
> in prayer for your intention, why not go to a
> saint in heaven who is already purified and
> perfected and sees the face of God? Our
> brothers and sisters in Heaven have already
> been sanctified, so why can't we ask for them
> to pray for our specific intentions?

We believe in giving honor to the communion of saints
in heaven. One way, aside from directly praying to them, is by
wearing medals with their images, and displaying statues and
pictures of them in our homes. Again, we do these things as
visual reminders of these wonderful saints who are just waiting

for us to call upon them and their powerful intercession. When we display a small statue of St. Michael the Archangel on an altar or in a child's room, we are reminded of his courage in rejecting Lucifer and fighting the good battle for Christ. We can feel his powerful intercession and presence as protection against evil. Any type of picture or image of the saints, angels, Blessed Mother or Christ serve as ways to bring our hearts, minds, and thoughts to God and godly things. There are so many distractions in our world today, we all need something visual during the course of our day to bring us back to God now and again. That is the purpose of having images and statues of the angels and saints.

Protestants may use the argument that having such images constitutes "worshipping false idols," but once again, this is a great misunderstanding.

We do not worship the actual stone that the statue is made from, nor the actual paper and frame from which a picture is made. Just as most of us have pictures of family members and loved ones around our homes, we have them as visual reminders of those we love. We do not actually worship the picture itself, but love and honor the friend or relative which the picture *represents*.

Help your children develop a personal relationship with specific angels and saints. Patron saints are a good place to start, but devise other ways in which your child may discover specific saints and learn to pray to them for intercession. Some ways are visiting saintly shrines, reading books about the lives of the saints and watching television program on the lives of specific saints on Catholic programming networks.

Teach your children that the saints and angels in heaven, and the souls in purgatory, are all a part of the

Church. We ask them for their intercessory prayers because we are all members of this same Church. We hope to join the saints in heaven some day to be a part of the Church Triumphant. Until then, we will ask them to pray for us and with us, because they are already blessed to see the face of God and their prayers are perfect.

## NOVENAS AND THE SAINTS

A novena is a prayer that you recite for a period of nine days (it can also be nine hours in some instances.) The purpose of a novena lies in the belief that we can draw on the immense intercessory power of the saints in heaven to pray both with us and for us for a particular intention. Perhaps the most common novena is said to St. Térèse of the the Little Flower. There are many novenas said to the Saints that are known to be especially helpful when invoked by the faithful for a particular purpose. (i.e. St. Anthony is the saint to pray to when you've lost something!)

In the appendix is a helpful list of Patron Saints of occupations, diseases and atates in life, along with their feast days.

# Some Final Thoughts . . .

As Catholic parents, we must be prepared to continually strive to learn our faith and internalize the truths it contains. Only when we have our own 'spiritual house in order' by fully understanding and grasping what the Catholic faith is all about will we be able to adequately teach it to our children. The more a child knows and comprehends about the fundamental truths of the One, Holy, Catholic and Apostolic Faith, the less likely it will be that he will leave the Faith as an adult. The huge number of Catholics who are falling away from the true Faith to join cults like The Jehovah's Witnesses and the Mormons, as well as those who are leaving the Faith to enjoy the often times 'feel-good' spirituality of the Protestant church down the street, are doing so because they probably do not fully know or understand their precious Catholic Faith.

It's critical that we help our children understand the riches of our Faith so that they do not leave it. It is also important for our children to understand what it means to be Roman Catholic. Clarify with your children from a young age that they are Catholic - and make the distinctions when questions arise about Protestant friends or relatives. I do not mean to foster a prejudism against Protestants.

Catholics must gladly acknowledge the esteem the truly Christian endowments for our common heritage which are to be found among our separated brethren. It is right and salutary to recognize the riches of Christ and virtuous works in the lives of others who are bearing witness to Christ...

—Decree on Ecumenism.

But we must not sugarcoat the truth: the Protestants do not share in the fullness of the Faith that we possess as Roman Catholics. We must ensure that our children understand the basic differences between Protestants and Catholics from a young age if the questions arise:

This person (so-and-so) is not Catholic like us. They are called 'Protestant.' That means that many years ago when the Church was split, some fell away and no longer are part of our Catholic Church. When part of the Church fell away (split), they changed many of the truths of the Faith and threw out other truths that they did not want to believe. They do not believe in our Pope, in honoring and praying to the Blessed Mother and Saints, in wearing saint's medals, in the Rosary, in the Eucharist or Confession, and many other truths which the Catholic Church teaches us. We do share some things in common with them: they love Jesus and believe in God the Father and the Holy Spirit, just like us. But you are very blessed, because we have given you the one, TRUE Faith. That is something that our Protestant friends don't have. They are missing a lot of it. It's kind of like this: the Catholic Faith is a full, perfect pie. The Protestants only have a little piece of this pie,

we Catholics have the whole pie! Think how
blessed you are to be Catholic and to have the
whole pie.

I've used this analogy to explain to my children the
distinctions between Catholics and Protestants when they
were asking things like, "Why doesn't so-and-so wear their
holy medals?" "How come so-and-so doesn't have any statues
of Mary in their home?", etc.

This book is meant to be a springboard for Catholic
parents to acquire a better grasp on some of the fundamentals
of our Faith. It is certainly not the only Catholic apologetic
book available. There are a large number of excellent works
which explore the topics I've presented here in more depth. If
this book has peaked your interest and left you wanting more,
please consider exploring some of the other fine apologetics
works, such as works by the eminent Karl Keating or Dr.
Scott Hahn.

See the appendix section which gives names of other
works you may wish to read, as well as fine apologetics
websites you may wish to visit on the internet.

This book is also intended to be a resource which
you can keep and to which you may refer in the future
when questions arise. You never know when your child will
approach with an unexpected question about the faith, a
well-meaning Protestant neighbor will ask a question about
our Catholic beliefs, or a non-Catholic relative may come
querying you with possible intentions of converting. The more
you know about our faith and the better grasp on its doctrines
and beliefs you have, the more our Lord will use you to bring
light to others who remain in darkness and outside the Faith.
The Catholic Faith truly has all the answers, we just have to
know where to find them.

# BIBLIOGRAPHY OF RESOURCES

St. Joseph Edition of The New American Bible: Catholic Book Publishing, Co., New York, 1992.

The Catholic Answers Tracts (online version): http://www.catholic.com/answers/tracts

The Catechism (online version) http://www.catholic.net/RCC/Catechism

The Catholic Encyclopedia, copyright 1913 by the Encyclopedia Press, Inc., Electronic version copyright 1996 by New Advent, Inc. http://www.csn.net/advent/cathen

Williams, Thomas David; A Textual Concordance of the Holy Scriptures, Tan Books and Publishers, Rockford, Illinois, 1985.

The Catechism of the Catholic Church, 1994, United States Catholic Conference Inc, -Libreria Editrice Vaticana.

Our Lady Teaches About Sacramentals and Blessed Objects, by Fr. Albert Joseph Mary Shamon, 1992, The Riehle Foundation.

## APPENDIX A

# THE PROTESTANT REVOLUTION

The term "Protestant" is a name generally given to those churches which broke away from the Catholic Church during the Reformation which began in the 1500's. It encompasses Lutherans, Anglicans, Presbyterians, Episcopalians, and Methodists. However, as of January 1997, it should be noted that there were more than 28,000 Protestant denominations, with dozens of new ones being formed weekly.

The Protestant Reformation began as a result of a number of reasons which will not be discussed in this brief appendix. If you'd like to explore the causes, you are urged to read more extensive explanations, such as that found in *The Catholic Encyclopedia*. The Reformation is recognized as being initiated by Martin Luther. He began by proclaiming the false doctrine of "justification by faith alone," but later denied most tenets of the Catholic Faith, including the Mass, sacraments, and the Papacy. He taught that the sole rule of faith must be the Bible, thus also rejecting the Sacred Tradition of the Church and the Teaching Magisterium.

In England, the Reformation was occurring for very different reasons. The tyrannical King Henry VIII was enraged when the Pope refused to recognize the King's invalid marriage to Anne Boleyn and severed his country from the Catholic Church. He declared himself the supreme judge in all church affairs and renounced any obedience to the Pope. This church, which still recognizes the King of England as its ecclesiastical head, is known as the Anglican Church, or Church of England.

One of the tragedies of the Reformation for the Protestants was that, for doctrinal reasons, seven books from the Old Testament and parts of two others were removed from their Bible. Therefore, the King James Version of the Bible, which is the standard Bible for most Protestants, is incomplete. The books of the Old Testament (1 and 2 Maccabees, Sirach, Wisdom, Baruch, Tobit and Judith) and parts of Daniel and Esther, had been part of the authentic Canon of the Bible since the beginning of Church history. These books were omitted from the Protestant Bible largely because they contained doctrinal scriptural support for basic Catholic tenets (i.e. the Book of Maccabees refers often to Purgatory, which Protestants reject).

But, of course, the most tragic aspect of the Reformation is that it destroyed the unity of faith and the ecclesiastical organization of the Christian people of Europe and cut millions off from the true Catholic Faith.

*Source: The Catholic Encyclopedia, copyright 1913 by the Encyclopedia Press, Inc. Electronic version copyright 1997 by New Advent, Inc. http://www. knight.org/advent*

# Scapular Confraternity
*Short Formula of Blessing and Enrollment*

Priest: Show us, O Lord, Your mercy.

All: And grant us Your salvation.

Priest: O Lord, hear my prayer.

All: And let my cry come unto You.

Priest: The Lord be with you.

All: And with your spirit.

Priest: Let us pray:

All: O Lord Jesus Christ, Savior of mankind, by Your right hand sanctify † these Scapulars (this Scapular) which Your servants will devoutly wear for the love of You and of Your Mother, the Blessed Virgin Mary of Mt. Carmel; so that by her intercession, they may be protected from the wickedness of the enemy and may persevere in Your grace until death, Who lives and reigns forever and ever.

*The priest now sprinkles the Scapulars with Holy Water, after which he places one on each person, saying:*

Priest: Receive this Blessed Scapular and ask the Most Holy Virgin that, by her merits, it may be worn with no stain of sin and may protect you from all harm and bring you to everlasting life.

All:    Amen.

Priest: May Almighty God,

All:    Creator of Heaven and earth, bless † those whom He has been pleased to receive into the Confraternity of the Blessed Virgin Mary of Mount Carmel. We bet her to crush the head of the ancient serpent in the hour of their death, and, in the end, to obtain fro them a palm and the crown of Your everlasting inheritance. Through Christ our Lord, Amen.

*The priest now sprinkles*
*those enrolled with Holy Water.*

# DAILY RENEWAL TO THE TWO HEARTS

Most kind Jesus, humbly kneeling at Thy feet, we renew the consecration of our family to Thy Divine Heart. Be Thou our King forever! In Thee we have full and entire confidence. May Thy Spirit penetrate our thoughts, our desires, our words and our deeds. Bless our undertakings, share in our joys, in our trials and in our daily labors. Grant us to know Thee better, to love Thee more, to serve Thee without faltering.

By the Immaculate Heart of Mary, Queen of Peace, set up Thy kingdom in our Country. Enter closely into the midst of our families and make them Thine own through the solemn Enthronement of Thy Sacred Heart, so that soon one cry may resound from home to home: "May the Triumphant Heart of Jesus be everywhere loved, blessed and glorified forever!" Honor and Glory to the Sacred Hearts of Jesus and Mary!

Sacred Heart of Jesus, protect our family!

Most Sacred Heart of Jesus, Thy Kingdom come! Immaculate Heart of Mary, pray for our family! St. Joseph, friend of the Sacred Heart, pray for us! Our Patron Saints and Guardian Angels, pray for us!

(Say one Our Father, Hail Mary and Glory Be for the intentions of the Holy Father)

The parents may now bless their children. Make the sign of the cross on their foreheads saying, "May the blessing of Almighty God, the Father, the Son and the Holy Spirit, descend upon you and remain forever."

# LATIN AND EASTERN RITE CATHOLIC CHURCHES & PRIESTLY CELIBACY

M ost Catholic Churches in America are part of the Latin Rite, and are commonly known as Roman Catholic. There is another Rite known as the Eastern Rite Catholic Churches. This term refers to any Eastern Rite which is in union with the Pope and accepts him as the visible head of the Catholic Church, as well as accepts the whole repository of the Catholic Faith. Eastern Rite Catholics are known at Byzantine Catholics, Armenian Catholics or Maronite Catholics. The Eastern Rite Churches differ from our Latin Rite Roman Catholic Churches somewhat in that they have their own rites and patriarchs. However, they are considered true Catholics and are numbered with Latin Rite Catholics because they follow one and the same pope, celebrate the same valid sacraments, and believe the same tenets regarding faith and morals.

One of the differences in the Eastern Rite Catholic Church is that it allows a man to marry *before* ordination, but not after. The Bishops of the Eastern Rite, however, are required to be celibate. Once an Eastern Rite Catholic priest who is married becomes widowed, he is not permitted to remarry. However, in North America, the Eastern Rite clergy are required to be celibate, just as Latin Rite priests. The exception to this would be if the priest came from Eastern Europe and was already married.

Another exception to the celibacy rule in regards to Latin Rite Catholic clergy would be if a previously married Episcopalian, Lutheran, or other ministerial convert becomes ordained to serve in the Latin Rite Roman Catholic priesthood. This exception, which is rare but occurs occasionally, is called "Pastoral Provision". In such a case, the validly ordained Roman Catholic priest would be permitted to remain married.

*Source: The Catholic Encyclopedia, copyright 1913 by the Encyclopedia Press, Inc. Electronic version copyright 1997 by New Advent, Inc. http://www. knight.org/advent*

# PRAYERS

## EUCHARISTIC PRAYER TO BE SAID BEFORE COMMUNION

Dear Blessed Mother,

Our Lady of the Most Blessed Sacrament, please send your angels and saints to inspire everyone here today to receive Jesus in the Eucharist with true love and devotion. Dear Guardian Angel, please help me to approach the altar that I may receive the body, blood, soul and divinity of my Jesus with some sort of love and reverence similar to that of the Blessed Mother, saints and faithful who were devoted to Our Lord in the Blessed Sacrament My God, may I make a humble reception of this Eucharist to make reparation for all of the outrages, sacrileges and indifferences which are committed against my Eucharistic Lord anytime or anyplace. Amen.

## EXPECTANT MOTHER'S PRAYER
*(To be recited after receiving Holy Communion)*

Dear Jesus,

Thank you for coming to me in this Most Blessed Sacrament and for nourishing me with your Precious Body, Blood, Soul, and Divinity. Please allow this gift of yourself to also purify, strengthen, nourish and sanctify the child which grows within my womb. Please continue to allow my child to grow healthy and well until the day when this child will join our family. Amen.

## PRAYER FOR THE HOLY FATHER

O God, the Shepherd and Ruler of all the faithful, look down with favor upon Thy servant, Pope N, whom Thou hast deigned to appoint the supreme Pastor of Thy Church; grant, we beseech Thee, that both his word and example may benefit those over whom he has been placed, so that, together with the flock entrusted to his care, he may attain unto life everlasting, through Christ our Lord. Amen.

Most Sacred Heart of Jesus, pour in richest fullness Thy blessings upon Holy Church, the Pope, and all the clergy. Grant perseverence to the just, conversion to sinners, enlighten the unbelievers, bless our relatives, friends and benefactors; assist the dying, deliver the souls in Purgatory, and extend over all hearts the gentle dominion of Thy love.

Lord Jesus, shelter our Holy Father the Pope under the protection of Thy Sacred Heart. Be Thou his light, his strength, and his consolation. Amen.

# APPENDIX F

# OUR EUCHARISTIC LORD
*A Guide for Young Children*

Q. What is the Eucharist?

A. The Eucharist is the gift of the Body and Blood of Jesus. We receive this gift when we receive Jesus in Holy Communion.

Q. Who gave us the Eucharist?

A. Jesus gave us the gift of himself in the Eucharist for the first time at the Last Supper, the night before he was crucified. He celebrated the Last Supper with his friends, the twelve apostles.

Q. What did Jesus say at the Last Supper to give us the Eucharist?

A. Jesus told his apostles "Take this bread and eat it, this is my body." and "Drink from this cup, this is my blood." When Jesus said these special words, the bread and wine became His Body and Blood.

Q. Who has the power to give us the Eucharist today?

A. All Catholic priests have a special power given to them by Jesus which allows them to consecrate the bread and wine so that it becomes the Body and Blood of Jesus. In the Mass, the priest repeats the words which Jesus told his apostles at the Last Supper. When the priest says the words, "This is my Body" and "This is my Blood," a great miracle occurs. The bread and wine become the body and blood of Jesus. This miracle has a very long name: it's called 'transubstantiation.'

Q. Who else can change the bread and wine into the Body and Blood of Jesus?

A. Only a Catholic priest can change (consecrate) the bread and wine into the Body and Blood of Jesus.

Q. How can we eat the Body and Blood of Jesus?

A. When the miracle of transubstantiation happens at Mass, Jesus allows the bread and wine to still look and taste like bread and wine, but they are changed into the Body, Bood, Soul and Divinity of our Lord. Because the Body and Blood still look and taste like bread and wine, we can eat them.

Q. What can I do to show Jesus in the Eucharist that I love him?

A. When you enter and leave a Catholic Church, look for the hidden Jesus in the tabernacle and genuflect to Him. This shows Jesus that you believe He is in the Eucharist and you honor him.

When you pass a Catholic Church make the Sign of the Cross and say a little prayer to Jesus in the tabernacle. Even if you just say hello to Jesus, it will make Our Lord feel very happy that you took a moment to think about Him.

If you have a moment in your day, stop by your church and visit with the hidden Jesus in the tabernacle. Sit quietly for a few minutes and just talk to Him from your heart.

Q. What is Eucharistic Adoration?

A. Some Churches show their love for Jesus in the Eucharist by having Eucharistic Adoration. This means that the Consecrated Host which is Jesus is placed in a special holder called a 'Monstrance.' The Monstrance holds the Eucharist and is placed on an altar for people to come and visit.

Q. What should I do when I visit the hidden Jesus in the tabernacle or go to see Jesus in Eucharistic Adoration?

A. Just talk to Jesus like He is your best friend. Tell Jesus everything you are thinking about quietly in your heart. Ask Jesus to bless all of your family members, friends, neighbors, and relatives. Tell Jesus about anyone you know who is sick or has died. Tell Jesus all about your day. What was something good that happened that you want to share with Him? Also tell Jesus about anything bad that happened to you or about anything that you have done which you know may be wrong. Ask Jesus to help you know the things you do which hurt him, these are called 'sins.'

Q. How long should I visit with Jesus in the Eucharist?

A. Jesus is happy when you come to visit Him for any length of time. Even if you can only stop in for a minute, this will make Jesus very happy.

APPENDIX G

# PATRON SAINTS AND THEIR FEAST DAYS

| | | |
|---|---|---|
| Actors: | St. Genesius | (Aug. 25) |
| Architects: | St. Camillus de Lelllis | (July 18) |
| Art: | St. Catherine of Bologna | (Mar.9) |
| Artists: | St. Luke | (Oct. 18) |
| Athletes: | St. Sebastian | (Jan 20) |
| Authors: | St. Francis de Salles | (Jan 29) |
| Aviators: | Our Lady of Loretto | (Dec.10) |
| Bakers: | St. Elizabeth of Hungary | ( Nov. 19) |
| Barren Women (Infertility) | St. Anthony of Padua | (June 13) |
| Bodily Ills: | Our Lady of Lourdes | ( Feb. 11) |
| Cancer Patients: | St. Peregrine | (May 2) |
| Carpenters/Employment/Workers: St. Joseph | | (March 19) |
| Cooks: | St. Lawrence | (Aug. 10) |
| Deaf: | St. Frances de Salles | (Jan 29) |
| Dentists: | St. Apollonia | (Feb 9) |
| Desperate Situations: | St. Jude Thaddeus | (Oct. 28) |
| Dying: | St. Joseph | (March 19) |
| Expectant Mothers: | St. Gerard Majella | (Oct. 16) |
| Eye Trouble: | St. Lucy | (Dec. 13) |
| Farmers: | St. Isidore | (Mar. 22) |
| Firemen: | St. Florian | (May 4) |
| Gardeners: | St. Dorothy | (Feb. 6) |
| Headaches: | St. Teresa of Avila | (Oct. 15) |
| Heart Ailments: | St. John of God | (Mar. 8) |
| Hospitals: | St. Camillus de Lellis | (July 18) |
| Housewives: | St. Anne | (July 26) |
| Lawyers: | St. Ivo | (June 17) |
| Lost Articles: | St. Anthony of Padua | (June 13) |
| Lovers: | St. Raphael | (Oct. 24) |
| Mentally Ill: | St. Dymphna | (May 15) |
| Mothers: | St. Monica | (May 4) |
| Motorists: | St. Christopher | (July 25) |
| Musicians: | St. Cecelia | (Nov. 22) |
| Nurses: | St. Agatha | (Feb. 5) |
| Policemen: | St. Michael | (Sept. 29) |
| Poor: | St. Lawrence | (Aug. 10) |
| Postal Employees: | St. Gabriel | (Mar. 24) |
| Priests: | St. John Vianney | (Aug 9) |
| Printers: | St. John of God | (Mar. 8) |
| Protector of Crops: | St. Ansovinus | (Mar. 13) |
| Sailors: | St. Cuthbert | (Mar. 20) |
| Scholars | St. Brigid | (Feb. 1) |
| Scientists: | St. Albert | (Nov. 15) |
| Sick: | St. Philomena | (Aug. 11) |

## THE CATHOILC MOTHER'S RESOURCE GUIDE
by Maria Compton-Hernandez

In this small, easy to read book, Maria Compton-Hernandez, a Kansas mother of six shares her hints for living a 'practical spirituality'. It is intended as a way to help Catholic mothers find time in their busy, often hectic lives to develop and grow in their own spiritual lives within our Church. The ideas and examples, as well as a helpful resource list, are included in a way that makes them concrete and easy to implement.'                    $3.50

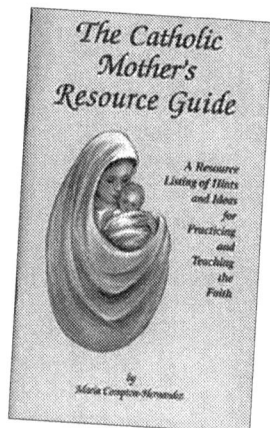

## CATHOLIC PARENTS INTERNET GUIDE
by Maria Compton-Hernandez

This exciting new book offers adult Catholics and easy-to-use guide to getting started on the internet. Beginning at square one, you will learn basics such as selecting an internet service provider and setting up an e-mail account. In no time you will be surrfing the web for the best Catholic information worldwide. Alsi includes instructions on blocking unwated sites from your children.        $4.95

**Call (412) 787-9735 or on-line at www.SaintAndrew.com**

# Help Spread the 'Queen of Peace' Newspaper!

## Secret of Fatima Edition
This 2001 edition takes a closer look at the Secret of Fatima, and in particular, the 'Third Secret' which was revealed by the Church on June 26, 2000. Included is the commentary written by Cardinal Ratzinger, which accompanied the secret's release.

## Afterlife Edition
This edition examines the actual places of Heaven, Hell and Purgatory through the eyes of the Saints, Mystics, Visionaries, and Blessed Mother herself. Will you be ready come judgment day?

## Illumination Edition
This edition focuses on a coming 'day of enlightenment' in which every person on earth will see their souls in the same light that God sees them. Commonly referred to as the 'Warning' or 'Mini-Judgment', many saints and visionaries, particularly the Blessed Mother have spoken about this great event, now said to be imminent.

## Eternal Father Edition
This edition makes visible the love and tenderness of God the Father and introduces a special consecration to Him. Many of His messages for the world today tell of the great love He has for all of His 'Prodigal Children.'

## Holy Spirit Edition
This edition reveals how the Holy Spirit continues to work through time and history, raising up great saints in the Church. Emphasized in the hidden, yet important role of Saint Joseph.

## Eucharistic Edition
This edition contains evidence for the Real Presence of Christ in the Eucharist. Many miracles and messages are recorded to reaffirm this truth.

## Special Edition III
This edition focuses on the great prophecies the Blessed Mother has given to the world since her apparitions in 1917 at Fatima. Prophetic events related to the 'Triumph of Her Immaculate Heart' are addressed in detail.

## Special Edition II
This edition examines the apparitions of the Blessed Mother at Fatima and in relation to today's apparitions occurring worldwide.

## Special Edition I
The first in a trilogy of the apparitions and messages of the Blessed Mother, this edition tells why Mary has come to earth and is appearing to all parts of the world today.

www.ingramcontent.com/pod-product-compliance
Lightning Source LLC
Chambersburg PA
CBHW031518040426

42445CB00009B/289